THE WATER FOWL
OF
INDIA AND ASIA

THE WATER FOWL

OF

INDIA AND ASIA

FRANK FINN, B. A. (OXON), F.Z.S., M.B.O.U.

GYAN

Published by

Gyan Publishing House
5, Ansari Road
Daryaganj, New Delhi-110002
Phone: 011-47034999, 9811692060
E-mail: books@gyanbooks.com

Distribution Network
gyanbooks.com
India, USA, Canada, UK, Australia, France

ISBN: 978-81-212-8648-0 (PB)
First Published, 1909

2nd Impression 2023

Printed at: Gyan Press, Delhi.

THE WATER FOWL OF INDIA AND ASIA
Author: FRANK FINN

(Page 72) H. Grönvold, del.

Comb-duck.

THE WATER FOWL

OF

INDIA AND ASIA

BY

FRANK FINN, B.A. (OXON), F.Z.S., M.B.O.U.,

Late Deputy Superintendent of the Indian Museum,

AUTHOR OF

"*Garden and Aviary Birds of India,*" "*How to know the Indian Waders,*" "*Ornithological and other Oddities,*" "*Birds of the Countryside,*" "*The World's Birds,*" "*Fancy Waterfowl,*" "*Fancy Pheasants,*" *&c., &c.*

CALCUTTA: THACKER, SPINK & Co.

1909

PREFACE TO THE SECOND EDITION.

THE favourable reception which the Anglo-Indian public has been kind enough to accord to the present work in its first form "How to know the Indian Ducks" has been deemed a justification for the issue of this revised edition, which has not only been brought up to date as far as Indian waterfowl are concerned, but amplified by the addition of brief notices and descriptions of all non-Indian Asiatic species. Thus the book is now a complete guide to all the wild fowl of Asia from the Mediterranean to the Pacific, and will, it is hoped, be serviceable to sportsmen East and West of our Indian Empire, as well as affording means of identification to Anglo-Indians of species at present not known as Indian, but likely in the future to come over our borders, as the Red-breasted Goose and Mandarin Duck have done since the publication of this work in its original form.

By way of keeping to the original plan of a work of reference for Anglo-Indians especially, however, the matter dealing with non-Indian Asiatic species has been kept in small print, and these species are not included in the keys, to simplify matters as much as possible. The majority of the ducks the sportsman is likely to meet with, it must be remembered, are found all across Asia in greater or less abundance, so that if he knows the Indian species he will be well advanced in his knowledge of those he may meet with in shooting elsewhere in Asia; or in Europe either, for that matter.

By way of making the work as useful as possible to beginners, the drawings of heads which have now been added—the work of that most accurate artist, Mr. H. Grönvold,—have been selected so as to illustrate the commoner kinds of ducks, etc., and include all those most likely to fall to the gun in ordinary Indian shooting.

F. FINN.

LONDON, 1909.

PREFACE TO THE FIRST EDITION.

"HOW TO KNOW THE INDIAN DUCKS."

THE present little work is substantially a reprint of a series of articles, which appeared in the *Asian* from November 1898 to June 1899, with a few additions and alterations; and I am much indebted to Mrs. Targett, the proprietress of that journal, for permission to reproduce the series in book-form.

My excuse for doing so is, that having for years taken an interest in the birds with which it deals, and having had, from my connection with the Indian Museum and my opportunities of keeping an eye on the Calcutta market, the privilege of recording during the past six years an usual number of rarities, I have felt impelled to put before the public a little handbook which may prove useful to those who are less fortunately situated. I can at least claim, I think, to have made my diagnoses simple and plain, and to have succeeded in keeping almost entirely free from technical terms.

The General Synopsis of the Indian Ducks, which forms Appendix I, and the Index of the work, is more than has been attempted by any previous writer in this field; and the succeeding Table of colours of Full-plumaged Males, if read with any attention, should serve the purpose of the identification of such nearly as well as a series of plates; for young birds and females, even plates are hardly sufficient without diagnoses or descriptions.

I must, in conclusion, express my obligations to the writers of other works dealing with this subject, and in especial to Messrs. Hume and Marshall's invaluable *Game Birds of India, Burma, and Ceylon;* Dr. W. T. Blanford's fourth volume on Birds in the *Fauna of British India* series, the nomenclature of which is followed in the present book; and Mr. E. C. S. Baker's series of articles on *Indian Ducks and their allies*, in the Journal of the Bombay Natural History Society. In addition, I have been indebted for pieces of information to several friends, whose names mostly appear in the course of the work.

F. FINN,

April, 1901. *Indian Museum, Calcutta.*

CONTENTS.

CHAPTER I.

CHAPTER II.

CHAPTER III.

CHAPTER IV.

CHAPTER V.

APPENDIX III.

ILLUSTRATIONS.

THE WATER FOWL

OF

INDIA AND ASIA.

CHAPTER I.

INTRODUCTION.

THERE is no more generally interesting group of birds than the family *Anatidæ*, which includes the Ducks and their allies the Swans, Geese and Mergansers; and certainly there is none in India, or in most other countries either, better fitted to attract to the study of general ornithology those hitherto unacquainted with its charms. So many species occur in our area; they differ so interestingly in their habits; their plumage is often so striking or so delicately beautiful; and last, but not by any means least, they are all fit, and some very good, to eat. I say nothing of the sport to be obtained from shooting them, for to most people that will be the leading motive for making their acquaintance at all; though, from another aspect which has been too little studied, both by ornithologists and by the general public, Ducks are not unworthy of attention. Given only a little pond, no birds are so easy to keep as pets; they can be allowed to run even in a garden, and are generally both hardy and peaceable, while requiring the minimum of attention. They seem to be invariably popular in public gardens, and I do not understand why they have not to a greater extent engaged the attention of amateurs of birds. Out here, of course, the unsettled habitation of many of us forbids much keeping of pets, but to the retiring Anglo-Indian, or to him whose lines are cast in one place for his whole service, I can cordially recommend the "waterfowl fancy," if he cares for birds at all.

Returning to Ducks as game, the pleasure of making a bag is much enhanced, to any one who knows his birds, by the possibility of securing a rarity, which is particularly great in the case of Ducks. I do not think that the record of rare "occurrences" is by any means the highest form of ornithology; but out here the pursuit of it is at least not harmful, as it too often is at home, and is indeed important, seeing the vast area we have to deal with. And any extensive Duck-shooting, or even searching a market or native fowler's catch, is likely to result in some "find" of value to the naturalist.

How to Distinguish a Duck.

Having said this much by way of introduction, we may proceed to the means of distinguishing a Duck when the bird has been obtained by means legitimate or otherwise. Most people know a Duck or Goose at sight, but there are exceptions, and for the sake of these weak brethren, I must ask those whose knowledge is greater to excuse what will seem to them unnecessary details. I have heard of one sportsman exhibiting a Cormorant, and another a Coot, as a Duck; and as Dabchicks have been offered to me in the Calcutta bazaar as Teal, I presume that particular "sell" has been worked successfully on others.

A Duck then (and the word "Duck" shall, as our legal friends would say, in this connection be taken to refer to and include all Teal, Geese, Swans and Mergansers) can be distinguished from all other Indian birds by the following characters :—The bill is *straight* and armed at the edges of both chaps (*mandibles*) with a row of transverse ridges or teeth (*lamellæ*), and the feet have moderate or short shanks (*tarsi*) and three toes in front webbed together, and a small, nearly or quite useless toe behind, not connected with the front ones by a web.

It may be as well to point out how these characters exclude all pretenders to the dignity of Ducks. *Coots, Phalaropes or Swimming Snippets, and Dabchicks and other Grebes*, are at once excluded, not only by their beaks, which are not in the least like a Duck's, but especially by their feet, of which the toes are not webbed together, but provided each with a separate and individual web.

Flamingoes have ridged beaks like Ducks, but the beak is bent suddenly downwards in the middle, and the shanks are very long.

Cormorants, Pelicans and their allies, not only have not the ridged beak but the hind toe is well developed, and joined to the front ones by an extension of the web which unites these.

Gulls, Terns and Petrels have a plain-edged beak, though their feet are very like those of Ducks, except that in the last the hind toe is reduced to a nail only.

As for those birds which swim, though without any web to their feet, such as Moorhens, no one has any business to mistake them for Ducks at all.

General Account of the Ducks.

Before proceeding to distinguish the various sections of the Duck family, a little more about its general characteristics may be noted. The most marked peculiarity about the Duck's bill is of course its ridged edges; this ridge arrangement presenting, as was pointed out by Darwin, a beautiful gradation in various species from simple teeth to processes so long that they fairly represent whalebone in miniature. This is well seen in the bill of the Shoveller, along the edges of which there is a regular comb. The bill is covered with skin, not with horn as in most birds, except at the end, where there is a "nail" which takes up more or less of the tip, and is often coloured differently from the rest of the bill.

The body is heavy, the tail generally short, rounded or pointed, composed of many feathers, much hidden at the root by the thick soft coverts, and the wings are never excessively long, and often markedly short; but all Indian species can fly, except in the moulting season, when, as with members of this family in general, all the wing-quills are shed at once. But as most of our water-fowl come to us as winter migrants, they have to get over their wing-moult before they start on their journey south.

Most of our Ducks also breed in Central and Northern Asia, making a nest on the ground which they line with their own down. Our resident Indian Ducks mostly build in trees as a rule, and the downy lining to the nest is imperfect or wanting.

The eggs of the Ducks are numerous, and white, pale buff or green in colour, without spots. The young, as every one knows, are active and feed themselves, and are clothed in hairy-looking down. They get well fledged on the body before the wing-quills are grown, and in this stage are known as "flappers." Their first plumage generally resembles that of the old female, but may differ from that of either parent.

Although Ducks are monogamous in the wild state, and often show considerable conjugal devotion, they readily take to polygamy in domestication, and hybridize freely. Even among wild birds hybrids are not uncommon, though, curiously enough, such seem seldom to occur in India. Mr. Hume says nothing about them in his "Game Birds and Wildfowl," and I have personally seen very few Indian specimens. It is hardly credible, however, that many hybrids do not really visit us, and the possibility of finding one of these curious crosses gives an additional interest to the study of the group.

As food, Ducks vary very much, the difference depending to a certain extent on what they have themselves previously eaten. The worst may, at a pinch, be improved for the table by skinning them, the unpleasant flavour largely residing in the skin, which is loaded with fat in these birds.

Distribution of the Ducks.

Ducks are found all over the world, most of the finest forms, however, living, or at any rate breeding, outside the topics ; few species reside constantly in India or other hot countries. The number of migratory Ducks that visit the Indian Empire in the cold weather, however, bring up our number of species to nearly a fourth of the whole family.

It will be noticed that the non-Indian species occurring in Asia are nearly all high northern birds, and often of marine habits, and the lines of migration followed by these are not likely to take them to India as a rule, though they are liable to occur there, as such maritime species as the sheldrake, golden-eye, and scaup do so.

As Asia, zoologically considered, extends down through the East Indies to Bali, it has been necessary to include the descriptions of a few East Indian species, most of which are properly Australian forms which extend westwards. Of the Asiatic Ducks, on the other hand, hardly any reach Australia.

Divisions of the Duck Family.

So far I have spoken of " Ducks " in a general sense, as I warned my readers above ; but there and at the beginning I mentioned that under *Anatidæ* came also the birds known as Swans, Geese and Mergansers and these groups, together with the birds to which the name of Duck is usually restricted, form four obvious sub-divisions of the family; these sub-divisions are adopted by Dr. Blanford in the fourth Bird Volume of the *Fauna of British India* series as the "sub-families" into which the *Anatidæ* are divided by him—an arrangement which is very simple and easy to follow. But how about Teal ? will probably be asked. In answer to this it can only be said that the word "Teal" simply means a small Duck, and has been generally so used, just as big Ducks have frequently attained to the dignity of "Geese" both with naturalists and with the general public. It will prove more convenient in the long run, however, to restrict these words to the birds to which they most properly belong, and with Indian birds this can generally be done.

As to the distinction of the four groups of the Ducks, this is not difficult with Indian species, if certain obvious characters be attended to.

SWANS (*Cygninæ*) are at once distinguished by their exceedingly long necks and by their great size, exceeding that of an ordinary tame Goose. The plumage is white or grey, according to age.

GEESE (*Anserinæ*) differ from most other Indian members of the Duck tribe in having the front edge of the nostrils about the middle of the beak, instead of nearer the root than the tip, according to the usual rule among Ducks and birds in general. Their plumage is plain grey or brown with lighter edges, giving it a barred appearance. This will at once prevent the Golden-eye Duck, which is pied, from being mistaken for a Goose, though unlike other Ducks, it has nostrils set far forward, much as in a Goose. Geese are of large size as a rule, but no Indian wild Goose is so big as an ordinary tame one. This excludes the Whooper Swan, which is much bigger than a tame Goose, but has the nostrils about the middle of the beak.

MERGANSERS (*Merginæ*), being a small group, may be taken next in order. They are to be known from other Indian *Anatidæ* by their narrow tapering bills, more than twice as broad at the root as at the tip, which at first sight do not seem to belong to birds of this family at all, the broad flat round-tipped bill being such an obvious difference between Ducks and any other birds. Their plumage is pied.

THE TRUE DUCKS (*Anatinæ*), which are very much in the majority, form the rest of the family. They have none of the peculiarities which distinguish the others, and are hence chiefly distinguishable by negative characters. The biggest of them is nothing like as big as a tame Goose, and they are generally smaller than a wild one; their necks are only moderately long, their nostrils (except in the Golden-eye) are always nearer the root of the beak than the tip; and the beak itself, though it varies in width and is sometimes narrowed towards the point, never approaches the *markedly* narrow and tapering form of that of the Mergansers.

CHAPTER II.

Swans.

Only two Swans are known to occur within our limits, and of these one is rare, and the other has only been found twice, so that a Swan is not a very probable item in an ordinary bag.

In addition to their large size and very long necks, Swans possess the following noticeable characters :—Their beak is very much like that of an ordinary Duck in form, long, parallel-sided and flat, with the ordinary ridges along the sides, and a moderate-sized " nail." The space between the eye and bill (*lores*) is bare in full-grown birds, and forms a noticeable peculiarity. The head is comparatively small, the body large and the wings broad ; the legs are set far back, with short shanks and large feet, the middle toe being longer than the shank, and the outer toe also long.

Swans are essentially surface-water-birds ; they do not frequent the land much, and when there walk ungracefully ; on the water they swim well and strongly, but do not dive (at any rate as far as I have seen) ; by means of their length of neck they can reach food some distance below the surface. The tame species, and no doubt the wild ones also, will turn " end up " like a Duck when feeding in deeper water than the length of the neck is sufficient to fathom. They rise with difficulty, running along the water for some distance, but when well on the wing fly faster than they appear to do. In their food, Swans are omnivorous, like Ducks, devouring small aquatic animals, fish, spawn, grain, and green land and water herbage, especially the latter.

Their nest is a large structure, built upon the ground, and it has been observed with the tame species that the bird is continually anxious to raise it, as if always haunted by dread of a flood.

The parents defend the nest vigorously, their wings being the chief weapons in fighting, for the Mute Swan at all events has very little power in the bill. I have let a vicious old male in the London Zoo, years ago, chew away at the back of my hand as much as he liked, and he could hardly graze the skin.

Both male and female are alike in their pure white plumage, the former being rather larger in size ; the young differ from both in being of a dull brownish grey, with less brilliantly-coloured beaks than their parents. The feet are black or dark grey in old birds at all events. Both of our species are much of a size, and the distinctive characters are mainly to be sought in the form and colour of the bill.

The *Mute* or *Tame Swan* may be distinguished at all ages by having the front edge of the nostril nearer to the root of the bill than to the tip ; while the *Whooper*, like a goose, has the front edge of the nostril about the middle of the beak.

The Mute or Tame Swan.

Cygnus olor, BLANFORD, Faun. Brit. Ind., Birds, Vol. IV, p. 413.

VERNACULAR NAMES. (No special name exists, but Hume says that in the N.-W. Punjab Swans are known by the name *Penr*, this being usually applied to Pelicans.)

The Mute Swan has, when *adult*, a knob at the base of the bill, which is orange-red, the nail, nostrils, edges, knob and triangular bare space between bill and eye being black. The *female* has a smaller knob than the male. In the *young bird* there is at first hardly any knob to the bill, the ground-colour of which is dark grey, while the bird is in the sooty brownish grey plumage of the first autumn ; as the plumage becomes white, the bill turns to a lighter grey tinged with green, and before the close of the second year, at which time the bird has become white, the grey tint of the beak has given place to a pinkish flesh-colour, which, in the following spring, darkens into the full orange-red. Face-skin always black. Nostrils nearer root of bill than tip.

In the variety known as the Polish Swan, which is either a case of albinism or of precocious maturity, the plumage being white or nearly so from the first, the bill is pale purplish pink in the young, not grey. This looks as if precocity were the true explanation.

The Mute Swan inhabits the greater part of Europe, Northern and Central Asia, migrating south to some extent in winter, when it visits Northern Africa regularly, and India occasionally. Twice, however, these birds have been killed near Peshawar, a good locality for Swans, in June and July. This Swan is one of the most familiar ornamental birds in Europe, and as it is only semi-domesticated, often looking after itself entirely, it frequently, when left unpinioned, takes wing ; and hence the natural limits of the wild birds in Europe are rather difficult to settle with accuracy. It is said to have been introduced into England by Richard Cœur-de-Lion, that country not being part of its natural range. This swan lays—according to the age of the female—from five to eight eggs, which are greenish grey in colour.

Swans are often imported into India and command a high price ; possibly the summer-killed Indian bird above alluded to were only "escapes" after all.*

* The Black Swan of Australia (*Chenopis atratus*) has been, however, far more numerously brought over, and as it has bred in this country, and escaped, is not unlikely to occur wild. Its black plumage, with white quills and red bill, will of course at once distinguish it from all Indian wild-fowl.

The late Mr. W. Rutledge, the well-known Calcutta dealer in animals, used to import two or three dozen yearly for many years, and some have got away to his knowledge. But Mr. Hume says it is mostly the birds of the year which occur in India. These would be mainly grey in plumage and in this stage will be found fit for food. The head, or even the skull, if preserved, will be sufficient for identification of the species. The breeding habits of this Swan in Europe are well known ; the nest is large, the eggs, from about a dozen to half that number, are white or nearly so. The male jealously guards his home, and his majestic appearance when roused in its defence is well known ; this graceful attitude with arched neck laid back, and secondary wing feathers raised, being, however, assumed at other times.

The Mute Swan, as its name implies, is a very silent bird, uttering ordinarily only a nasal croak, or when angry, a hiss.

The whole length of the bird is about 5 feet, and that of its closed wing (from knuckle to end of longest quills) about 2 feet.

The Whooper or Wild Swan.

Cygnus musicus, BLANFORD, Faun. Brit. Ind., Birds, Vol. IV, p. 114.

VERNACULAR NAMES.—None known.

The Whooper has no knob on the bill at any age ; when the bird is *adult*, this is black for about the tip half, the rest being bright yellow, which colour also extends to the bare skin of the face.

In the *young* the beak is dull flesh-colour at first, with black edges and tip ; then, while the birds are still grey, the end becomes black, and the root and face greenish-white, with a reddish-orange band across the nostrils.

At the close of the second year, when the plumage, as in the other species, has become white, the bill has assumed its full colour of yellow and black.

In size it is about equal to the Mute Swan, but has a longer bill, about four inches in length.

Thus the light face will always distinguish the Whooper, in addition to the difference in the position of the nostrils, which in this species are in the middle of the bill. The tail also in the Whooper is shorter and rounded, while in the Mute Swan it is longer and pointed.

The Whooper is a more northern species than the Mute Swan, breeding in high latitudes in Europe and Asia, and wintering in the greater part of the former Continent, and in the temperate regions of the latter. It has only thrice been found in India. Hodgson obtained a specimen in the Nepal Valley in January 1829. This, or rather its skull and foot, had been referred by Mr. Hume to the smaller species *Cygnus bewicki*; but Blanford regarded the relics as undoubtedly pertaining to a Whooper. No other specimen as was recorded till 1900, when Lieutenant-General W. Osborn, I.S.C., shot one out of a flock of four on the River Beas on January 6th. Also, on January 31st, 1904, Mr. J. Crerar shot one on the Changra Dhand in Sind.

The Whooper is a much greater vocaliser than the other species; it has, indeed, a very fine trumpet-like call. It walks better on land, and a winged bird will make a good run for its life, and has even been known to charge when overtaken. On the water, however, this species does not equal the Mute Swan in beauty, as it carries its neck straight and does not raise its wings. The light yellow face also, and knobless beak, completely deprive the Wild Swan of the haughty and dignified air of its rival. It lays four to six yellowish white eggs.

The windpipe in this species is much elongated and coiled, the coils being lodged in the keel of the breastbone.

Bewick's Swan.

Cygnus bewicki, SALVADORI, Brit. Mus. Cat., Birds, Vol. XXVII, p. 29.

Is very like the Whooper, but decidedly smaller, and has the yellow on the base of the bill less extensive, and terminating rather abruptly; it does not reach the basal end of the nostril, whereas in the Whooper the yellow runs on below the nostril and ends in a point.

This species has much the same range as the Whooper, but does not breed so far west in Europe, though visiting Britain in winter. Like the Whooper, it is found in China and Japan at that season, and although not yet known to occur in India, will probably be found to do so, sooner or later. The eggs are like the Whooper's, but smaller. The bill in this species is little over three-and-a-half inches long, and the shank barely four, while the closed wing is about a foot-and-a-half. The total length is about four feet.

Pere Davie's Swan.

Cygnus davidi, SALVADORI, Cat. Birds, Brit. Mus., Vol. XXVII.

Is a very mysterious bird, only one specimen being on record, which was seen by that excellent ornithologist, Swinhoe, in the Museum of the Lazarist Mission at Pekin in 1868; the specimen had been bought in the market at Tientsin.

It was smaller than Bewick's Swan and was all white with red bill tipped with a black nail, and orange-yellow feet.

No other specimen has since been obtained, and it is just possible that the specimen seen by Swinhoe was one of an expiring species, which has now disappeared altogether. It must not be forgotten that a conspicuously coloured diving-duck (*Camptolœmus labradoricus*) formerly well known in North America, has completely disappeared in our time, and there are not nearly so many specimens of it in Museums as there are of the Great Auk.

CHAPTER III.

Geese.

Our certainly ascertained Indian Geese are five in number, and form a group of birds very easily recognizable even to the beginner.

In addition to the central position of the nostrils in the bill, Geese present so many other notable peculiarities that they are really very easy to distinguish. The difference between a Goose and a Swan is proverbial, and it is rather curious that any true Ducks should have been able to claim rank as Geese as they have done.

All our Geese, then, have the following characteristics in common ; a rather long neck, bearing a comparatively small head, provided with a beak shorter and narrower than is usual in the family, and very high at the root while sloping rapidly to the point, so that the bill, as a whole, has a conical form. The armature of its edges is in the form of teeth, and the nail is generally large, taking up the whole of the tip ; the whole organ being thus admirably adapted for cropping grass and other herbage. The nostrils, as above stated, are nearly central, the body is less heavy than is usually the case among Ducks, the wings are long and broad, and the tail is rounded.

The legs are rather long, the shank being about as long as the middle toe, and are set well forward.

The plumage is very characteristic, grey or brown in colour, with the edges of most of the feathers, which are broad and blunt, lighter, so that the general effect is one of transverse barring ; the quills are dark, at any rate at the end, and the stern and feathers at the root of the tail (*tail-coverts*) white ; the feathers of the neck are usually ridged or pleated.

The eyes are always dark, and the feet some shade of reddish or yellowish, never black or grey, as is often the case in our other *Anatidæ*. The colour of the beak and feet is more variable than is usual in birds.

Sauce for the goose is proverbially sauce for the gander, and they almost exactly resemble each other, though the former is usually rather smaller. Nor are the young very different from their parents in general appearance, though they often lack some of the characteristic marks of their species, and their feathers are narrower and more rounded than those of their parents.

In their habits and movements Geese are also very uniform. They are rather land than water-birds, though they swim well (being noticeably high in the stern on the water) and dive fairly ; but most of their time is spent on shore, where they walk well, though with a peculiar swaying gait, and can run fast and traverse long distances on foot if necessary. They occur in flocks if numerous.

Their flight is strong ; they rise readily, and can even perform various evolutions in the air, such as turning somersaults like a tumbler-pigeon. In feeding they are more strict vegetarians than most birds, living almost entirely on vegetable food, such as grass, roots and grain ; and when numerous, they may become terribly destructive to crops, not only by what they eat, but by trampling them down. They are themselves good food, if not equal to the best Ducks. They all breed outside India, to the north and west, building on the ground, and laying from six to a dozen eggs, yellowish white in colour.

Their voice is a cackle or a hiss, the latter when enraged, at which time the ludicrous appearance of the gander with gaping mouth and lowered neck, is well known. Both sexes have the same voice, and there is nothing peculiar about the structure of the windpipe in this sub-family.

The true Geese are all confined to the Northern Hemisphere, and even in winter do not go so far south as many of the Ducks.

Two species visit the Indian Empire commonly, the Gray and the Bar-headed, the other three being rare and occasional visitants.

The general appearance of these birds being, as above stated, uniform and unmistakeable, I shall endeavour in the descriptions to note only the salient points ; and I will try also to make the preliminary diagnosis of the species depend on characters which do not vary with age, so as to allow for the slight difference between the young and adults. We find then, that, of our six species :—

The *Bar-headed* is at once distinguishable by its pale clear grey colour, almost a French grey. The rest are brownish grey or brown, except the Red-breasted.

The *Red-breasted* is mostly black or very dark brown, with the breast chestnut or buff and the bill and feet black.

The *Dwarf*, as its name implies, is known from all the others, but the Red-breasted by its small size, which is only about that of a good big tame Duck, the bill being especially small, only about an inch and a half from corner of mouth (*gape*) to tip. All the other Geese but the Red-breasted have beaks of two inches or over.

The *Gray*, on the contrary, is the biggest bird of the lot, with a bill of two inches and a half or over, without any black on it.

The *White-fronted* has a two-inch bill, also without any black.

The *Pink-footed* is distinguished from all the rest by

(Page 17) H. Grönvold, del.

Gray Goose.

(Page 23) H. Grönvold, del.

Bar-headed Goose.

having the root of the bill black, the said bill being a two-inch one.

The Gray Goose.

Anser ferus, BLANFORD, Faun. Brit. Ind., Birds, Vol. IV, p. 416.

VERNACULAR NAMES.—*Sona*, *Kurria-sona Háns*, *Rajháns*, Hindi ; *Kar-háns*, Bhagulpur ; *Mogala*, *Mogala-battak*, Nepal Terai ; *Kangani*, Manipur.

The Gray Goose is the largest and most strongly built of the Indian species, with a big coarse bill well over two inches in length, with a strong nail and prominent teeth, shown plainly by the gaping edges. In colour it is generally of a brownish grey, some specimens being browner and others greyer. The " shoulder " of the wing is blue-grey, and so is the lower back ; the belly is more or less blotched with black in *old birds*. The bill and feet are fleshy pink, the colour varying in depth. The *young bird* has the lower back brownish-grey, and of course no black below. There is often a white patch on the forehead. The whole length is about two feet and a half, and the closed wing about one-and-a-half, bill two-and-a-half inches or over ; shank three inches.

In Europe the Gray Goose often has an orange bill, but apparently never in India ; there, however, according to Mr. Hume, the colour of the bill and feet varies much in intensity, from creamy white hardly tinged with pink to dingy livid purplish red. These differences, he thinks, are matters of individual complexion, as he did not find them dependent on season ; but, on the other hand, often coinciding with differences in the general tone of plumage so variable in this species. I may add that the bills and feet of waterfowl vary much in intensity of colour according to the state of health of the bird, being pale when it is not in good form. Moreover, I have observed that in captive birds of this species kept in the Calcutta Zoo, the beak varied from rose-red in the spring to a sallow flesh-colour when the birds were moulting, so there is evidently some seasonal change depending on vigour. I have seen one or two specimens in which the "nail" at the tip of the bill, usually white, was horn-colour, but it never approached black.

The Gray Goose breeds in Europe north of about 50° latitude, and in Central Asia and Southern Siberia, wintering in South Europe, North Africa, South-Western Asia, and Northern India. It is especially common in the cold weather in the Punjab, Sind, and the North-West Provinces, and occurs also in Assam, Burma, and Manipur.

It is found as far south as the Nerbudda on the West, and the Chilka Lake in Orissa on the East; but seldom south of the Gangetic plain inland. It is often in very large flocks, from two hundred to a thousand birds or more, but the total number of birds that visit India is not, in Mr. Hume's opinion, more than a fifth of that of the Bar-headed, to be mentioned below.

This species is the original stock of the Tame Goose of Europe, and was already domesticated, and sometimes at least white, in the time of Homer, as we know from certain passages in the Odyssey. It ought, however, to be mentioned that there is some possibility of the White-fronted Goose, to be dealt with hereafter, having had a share in the origin of our tame birds. The Goose has varied very little during these long ages of domestication in comparison with other birds more recently tamed, such as the fowl.

It should be mentioned, however, that the domestic Goose of India has sprung, at least in part, from a quite distinct species, the Chinese Goose (*Cygnopsis cygnoides*), to be noticed later.

It is usual to call the Gray Goose the Gray Lag, the latter word being supposed, with much reason, to mark out this species as the Goose which "lagged" behind to breed in Britain (as it formerly did, though now only doing so in a few places in Scotland) when the rest of the wild Geese went north. As, however, the "lag" is continually getting mixed up with "leg" and the bird's legs are anything but grey, I have thought it as well to drop this suffix, this species having the greyest plumage of all our Geese except the Bar-headed, which is well distinguished by the marking from which it takes its name.

The Pink-footed Goose.

Anser brachyrhynchus, BLANFORD, Faun. Brit. Ind., Birds, Vol. IV, p. 418.

VERNACULAR NAMES.—None known.

This Goose is smaller than the Gray, with a much shorter bill, but much resembles that species in colouring, though it is darker, but is easily distinguished from it and all our other Geese by its bill, which is black at the root and on the nail, the intermediate portion being pink, as are the feet. There is no black on the belly. The bird is about twenty-eight inches long; the closed wing about sixteen, and the bill two, shank three. Semi-domesticated birds have been known to produce young with orange band on the bill and orange feet, and specimens may also occur among wild birds; so that the black on the bill is the best character to go by. Such orange-billed and footed birds, did any turn up in India, might be mistaken for the Bean Goose (*Anser segetum*), which is strongly suspected of occurring here, and always has a black-and-orange bill and orange feet; but the former member is much larger than the bill of the Pink-footed Goose, being as big as in the Gray, about two-and-a-half inches, or even larger in some cases.

The Pink-footed Goose breeds in the extreme north of Europe, and chiefly visits the western part of that continent in water. It is rare in India, indeed, until recently the only Indian-killed specimen that had been *preserved* is one in the possession of Mr. Stuart Baker, which was obtained by a native collector in the south of Cachar. The occurrence of the bird had, however, been several times before recorded, and Mr. Hume had even got specimens, but these were lost. His birds, a pair, were shot in 1864, from a large flock of Grays among which their darker, browner colour and bright pink feet rendered them conspicuous. Specimens have also been procured of late years in the Shan States.

Sportsmen should, therefore, be on the look-out for this bird, and when found, make a note of it. It is found in pairs and small flocks, and appears to be very wild and wary.

The White-fronted Goose.

Anser albifrons, BLANFORD, Faun. Brit. Ind., Birds, Vol. IV, p. 417.

VERNACULAR NAMES.—None known.

This Goose when *adult* is of a general dark brown colour, with a white band across the forehead, extending to the corners of the mouth and sometimes the chin; the belly is more or less blotched with black, sometimes very heavily, the legs are orange, and the bill fleshy or yellow, with no black on it.

Young birds have no white on the head, or black on the belly. The bird is considerably smaller than the Gray Goose, being about twenty-seven inches long, with a wing of about fifteen; shank two and-a-half inches; bill two. This Goose has the widest range of all our Indian species, occurring in Europe, Asia and North America; for though the American form is sometimes distinguished as *Anser gambeli*, it appears to be hardly sufficiently distinct from our bird to rank as a full species; it is merely larger, with a bigger bill.

It breeds in high northern latitudes, migrating in winter to the coasts of the Mediterranean, Egypt, the Caspian Sea, Northern India, China and Japan. It is said to be found in Assam, and has been shot in Upper Burma. In America it reaches Mexico and Cuba in winter. With us it is a rare bird, visiting, in the cold weather, the Punjab, Sind, Cutch, Rohilkhand and Oudh, where it is usually found on rivers, singly or in very small parties of two or three birds. The note of this Goose resembles a laugh, whence it is sometimes called the Laughing Goose.

The Dwarf Goose.

Anser erythropus, BLANFORD, Faun. Brit. Ind., Birds, Vol. I, p. 418.

VERNACULAR NAMES.—None known.

This little Goose, which, as I said above, is only about as big as a large tame Duck, is very like the White-fronted; it has, however, proportionately longer wings and a smaller bill, is darker in colour (thus being the darkest of all our Geese), and has the white patch on the forehead in the form of a longitudinal "blaze" or broad streak, running up from the bill to the level of a line drawn between the eyes. The bill is pink or flesh-coloured (with no black), and the legs orange. The bill may apparently be sometimes orange or yellow. The eyelids are edged with lemon-yellow, and hence very conspicuous. *Young birds*, like the young of the White-fronted Goose, have no white on the head or black on the belly.

The length is about twenty-one inches, wing about fourteen, shank about two and-a-half, bill one and-a-half. The wings are thus proportionally much longer than in the White-fronted, or indeed than in any other of our Geese; when closed they reach well beyond the tail. The bird appears more compactly built than any other of our Geese.

The Dwarf Goose breeds in Lapland and eastwards also in Siberia; in winter it is found from Western Europe, where it is rare, to Northern India, China, where it is common, and Japan. It is a more Eastern bird than its larger ally the White-fronted; in India it is rare, less than a score of specimens having been taken.

This pretty little Goose, conspicuous among its kin by its small size and rich colouring, is probably more common than is supposed; for, during 1898, I got no less than four living birds from the Calcutta bazaar, a dealer there having imported them from up-country; three of these, fine old birds, I obtained on New Year's day, and one was exhibited alive before the Asiatic Society soon afterwards.

Two of them lived for some time in fine condition in the Alipore Zoo; the other with a younger bird subsequently obtained also among up-country birds in the bazaar, where I first noticed it in May of the same year, has died, and their skins are now in the Indian Museum, in poor condition unfortunately. Again, on January 7th, 1900, I saw, among a lot of up-country birds in the bazaar, yet another specimen of this species, rather younger than the rest; this was sold to go to England. This Goose has been observed to be very active in flight, as one might expect from its long wings.

The Bar-headed Goose.

Anser indicus, BLANFORD, Faun. Brit. Ind., Birds, Vol. IV, p. 419.

VERNACULAR NAMES.—*Háns*, *Kareyi Háns, Ráj Háns*, *Birwa*, H.; *Paria*, Nepal Terai; *Nang-pa*, Ladak; *Nir-bathu*, Tam.; *Badi-Háns*, Chittagong; *Káng-nai*, Manipur.

The Bar-headed Goose, the commonest of all our Geese, differs more from any of the rest than these do from each other; the bill has straighter edges and shows the teeth less, and has a smaller nail; the general build is lighter and more slender, so that, although the measurements are mostly about the same as those of the Gray, the bird is less bulky; and there is no pleating of the neck plumage, though this character may be absent in the Gray Goose. The colour of this species is equally characteristic, being a clear pale grey, passing into brown-grey on the neck and flanks; the head is white, with two black bars at the back, the first and longest reaching from eye to eye; and a white streak runs down each side of the neck. The bill is yellow or orange, with a black nail, and the legs are orange.

Young birds have the crown dark brown, and no black bars on the head or white stripes on the neck. The length is about thirty inches; the wing a foot and a half; the shank three inches, and the bill about two.

The Bar-headed Goose breeds in Tibet and Central Asia, visiting India in winter far more numerously than any other Goose, and being common in the north and rare in the south. It occurs in Manipur, and is common on the Irrawaddy and elsewhere in Upper Burma. But it is rare in the Bombay Presidency, and unknown on the Malabar Coast. It is found in small or large flocks. It is a far more graceful bird, both on land and water, than the Gray, our only other common Goose, walking more easily and sitting higher in the water. It is according to Hume less tameable than that species, and does not stand the heat of the Indian summer so well, if kept in captivity, though this has not been my experience with this species at the Calcutta Zoological Gardens, where it certainly kept its condition perfectly.

The Red-breasted Goose.

Branta ruficollis, SALVADORI, Brit. Mus. Cat., Birds, Vol. XXVII.

VERNACULAR NAMES.—*Shakvoy*, in Siberia.

This beautiful little Goose has never been actually obtained in India, but it has been seen by so good an observer as Mr. E. C. Stuart Baker, and it is a very unmistakable bird, so I follow him in admitting it to our list.

It is a small bird for a Goose, not bigger than a large Duck and has a remarkably small delicate-looking bill for its size; the neck-feathering is not ridged or pleated.

The plumage is mostly black, with the front of the neck, and the breast, bright chestnut. There is a chestnut spot on the sides of the head, bordered with white, which white runs down the side of the neck. There is also a white patch between eye and bill; the flanks are barred black and white, and the belly and feathers at base of tail all white. The *young birds* are brown instead of black, and have the red of the neck and breast much paler, and the red patch on the sides of the head replaced by brown. The legs, bill, and eyes are all dark. This bird is about twenty-two inches long with the bill only about an inch, shank about two inches, and closed wing about fourteen inches. Conspicuous in its harlequin plumage of tortoise-shell and white, this hand some Goose has attracted attention from the remotest times, for a representation of it appears in what is the earliest bird-picture on record, from an Egyptian tomb of about 3000 B. C. In that part of the world, however, it is rare, though occurring as a straggler all over Europe, but its breeding home is in Western Siberia, and it migrates to Persia and Turkestan. Blyth believed that an old record of it in the long-defunct *Oriental Sporting Magazine* of 1836 referred to it, and as lately as March 1907 Mr. E. C. S. Baker actually saw five on the Brahmaputra, on which river Mr. Mundy had previously seen the species, and given a recognizable description of the birds to Mr. Baker.

Of the non-Indian Asiatic geese there are quite a number of species.

The Bean Goose.

(*Anser fabalis*, SALVADORI, Brit. Mus. Cat., Birds, Vol. XXVII, p. 99.)

This is a large goose, about equalling the GREY-LAG in size and with the neck-feathering similarly pleated, but not quite so heavily made ; in colour it is dark-brownish-grey, much browner than the GREY-LAG, and it has no grey on the "shoulder" of the wing. The bill, which is of a good size—very stout in some individuals—is black at the base and on the nail, and orange for the rest of its length. The amount of orange varies very much, as does the size and depth of the beak, especially the lower jaw. The legs are always orange, and the eyes dark.

The length is nearly a yard, with the closed wing nearly seven inches, the bill about two-and-a-half, and the shank nearly three ; but the size varies very much. This goose ranges across the Northern parts of the Old World, migrating south in winter ; it varies a great deal, and some authors divide it into several species, according to the size of the bill and the amount of orange on this. The most distinct of these races is MIDDENDORFF'S GOOSE (*Anser fabalis. Middendorfii*), which is a very large bird with the head and neck light buffy brown, occurring in Eastern

Siberia. Then there is SUSHKIN'S GOOSE (*Anser neglectus*) a form like the BEAN GOOSE, but with a weaker bill, and with a pink bar on this and pink feet, which might easily be confounded with the Pink-footed goose.

The Chinese Goose.

Cynopsis cygnoides, SALVADORI, Brit. Mus. Cat., Birds, Vol. XXVII, p. 107.

Is a large species, bigger than the gray, with long neck, with smooth plumage devoid of pleating, and with a large bill, flatter than is usual in geese, and inclined to be swollen at the forehead. This bill is entirely black, and the feet orange, a combination not found in any other goose. The plumage is of a lightish brown rather than grey, with the usual pale edgings to the feathers and white stern, but the most distinctive point about it is the dark-brown colour which covers the crown and runs down the back of the neck, contrasting sharply with the pale creamy colour of the rest of the head and neck. The total length of this goose is about a yard ; the bill is three-and-a-half inches long, shank three, and wing about a foot-and-a-half.

Everyone who knows the common domestic goose of India and China, which is descended from this species, will recognize this description, but the tame bird often has a very decided knob on the forehead, especially in the male, and is more coarse and paunchy in form than the wild type, besides being often white or pied. The wild home of the CHINESE GOOSE is Eastern Siberia, China, and Japan, and it may be expected to occur on our eastern frontiers in winter sometime or other.

Hutchins' Goose.

Branta hutchinsi, SALVADORI, Brit. Mus. Cat., Birds, Vol. XXVII, p. 114.

Like the BRENTS, next to be dealt with, belongs to a group with smooth necks and dark bills and feet, like the RED-BREASTED GOOSE. It is a rather small race of the well-known CANADIAN GOOSE of ornamental waters in Europe, now often found quite wild in Britain. It is about the size of the GREY-LAG, with the body-colour of a dark-brown with the usual light edges, the tail black, and the head and neck conspicuously glossy black with a white crescent on the throat, reaching up on the cheeks.

Its bill is rather over two inches long, and the shank three and-a-quarter ; the wing sixteen inches ; the total length is between two and three feet.

It is a North American bird chiefly but also found in North-East Asia, and visits Japan in winter.

The Brent Goose.

Branta bernicla, SALVADORI, Brit. Mus. Cat., Birds, Vol. XXVII, p. 119.

Kokugan of the Japanese.

Is a small species, about the size of a large duck, and very dark in colour, the head, neck, and breast quite black, with a white bar on each side close below the head. The stern is, however, white as in geese generally ; and the belly and flanks are smoky-grey, the latter more or less strongly marked with whitish tips to the feathers.

The length of this goose is about twenty-one inches, the bill about one-and-a-half, shank two, and closed wing just over a foot. It is a Northern bird, ranging from Europe to Eastern North America, and breeding in high latitudes : the four eggs it lays are creamy-white, and it builds near the sea, being purely a sea-bird, which feeds chiefly on sea-grass and other marine vegetation. On its winter migration it is found on the Japanese coasts. This is the chief wild-goose pursued by the gunner on British waters.

The Black Brent.

Branta nigricans, SALVADORI, Brit. Mus. Cat., Birds, Vol. XXVII, p. 123.

Is hardly more than a sub-species of the above, with the belly nearly as dark as the breast and the general tone of the back darker. The white neck-patches, however, meet in front. This is the characteristic BRENT of Western North America, but like the other, it visits Japan in winter.

The Snow Goose.

Chen hyperboreus, SALVADORI, Brit. Mus. Cat., Birds, Vol. XXVII, p. 84.

Haku-gan of the Japanese.

Belongs to a group with grooved or pleated featherings of

the neck, and the tertiary quills rather long and pointed. The teeth of the bill show very plainly.

The *adults* is pure white with black pinion-quills and rose-pink bill and feet. The *young* is grey, with the bill and feet dark greyish. The bill is about two-and-a-half inches long, shank three, and wing seventeen ; the total length rather over two feet. This is properly an Arctic American bird, but also occurs in North-Eastern Asia, and may be found in Japan in winter.

The Emperor Goose.

Philacte canagica, SALVADORI, Brit. Mus. Cat., Birds, Vol. XXVII, p. 109.

Is a very distinct species, stout and heavy in build, with very short bill and short shanks. Its plumage is clear grey, with each feather tipped first with black and then with white. The head and back of the neck are white, the throat down to the breast dark-brown. The bill is dark at the sides, pale flesh-colour down the centre, and the legs orange. *Young birds* are less clearly marked, and have the head and neck speckled. The bill is barely two inches long, the shank less than three, and the wing fifteen. The total length is rather over two feet. This little-known goose inhabits the northern shores of the Pacific on both sides. It is a sea goose, feeding on shellfish, sea-weeds, etc.

CHAPTER IV.

Mergansers.

The three species which compose this sub-family are at once to be distinguished, as above stated, by the form of the beak, which in all is markedly narrow, shallow, and tapering, being more than twice as broad at the root as at the tip. Its edges are armed with teeth, of which the upper row are plainly visible even when the bill is closed, and the large nail takes up the whole of the tip and forms a hook. The nostrils are nearer the root than the tip, as in ordinary Ducks.

It is practically only the peculiar bill which marks these birds off at all from the true Ducks (*Anatinæ*), and perhaps they hardly deserve sub-family rank, since, except for the form of the beak, they present no noteworthy distinction from the Golden-eye, which everybody would call a Duck. Still they have nearly always been given a separate position, and may retain it in this series.

Mergansers are about the size of or smaller than a tame Duck, and in general form, present a fair-sized head, a rather short neck, and a somewhat flat body. The wings are pointed, and if anything rather short, the tail rather long and rounded, and the feet are set far astern, with short shanks ; these being much exceeded in length by the middle toe, to which the outer toe is about equal, giving a large foot. The hind toe is furnished on its lower edge with a flap or lobe of skin.

The plumage of the Mergansers is pied, and very different in the two sexes, the males being black and white and the females grey, brown and white. The young resemble the female, and so does the male when in the undress plumage which he puts on for a time after breeding.

At the lower end of the male's windpipe there is a curious hollow enlargement, partly of bone and partly of membrane, the *bulla ossea* or drum ; and in the case of the Red-breasted Merganser, it has been noticed that in the pairing season the male alone emits a singular low hollow note. The ordinary voice of Mergansers is rather a croak than a quack.

Mergansers are swift and powerful swimmers and excellent divers, most of their time being spent on the water. On shore they move about very little, but are more active than most diving Ducks ; their flight is swift and powerful, though the Goosander rises with difficulty. They are the most carnivorous of the family, feeding on fish and other water animals, and regarded as food themselves are but indifferent, though probably edible enough if the skin be removed ; I have only tried the Red-breasted. Their nests are placed under cover, either in holes of trees or on the ground ; their eggs are numerous, and creamy or greenish white or buff in colour. One species, the Goosander, breeds within Indian limits in the higher Himalayas, migrating in winter to the base of the range ; but the other species, the Red-breasted Merganser and Smew, are migrants only, breeding to the northward of our area.

The Goosander and Smew are fairly common, but the Red-breasted Merganser is one of the rarest of Indian waterfowl, though probably commoner than is supposed.

The Goosander and Red-breasted Merganser very closely resemble each other and differ much from the Smew, for which reason these two are placed together in one group (*genus*), while the Smew, having no very near relative, occupies a genus by itself. The three birds are very easily distinguished by their beaks as follows :—

In the *Smew*, the beak is only about an inch-and-a-half long, and grey ; the beaks of the other measure between two and three inches, and are red, more or less dark along the ridge.

The *Goosander's* beak is shorter and thicker than that of the *Red-breasted Merganser*, and has fewer teeth, these numbering, in the upper chap, about fifteen between the nostril and the nail, while in the Red-breasted Merganser's longer and thinner bill there are about eighteen teeth between nail and nostril.

Besides the difference in length and colour of bill, the Goosander and Red-breasted Merganser agree with each other, and differ from the Smew, in the following points : The teeth of the bill point slantingly backwards, instead of being perpendicular as in the Smew ; the beak is much narrower, and has the nostril nearer the root than in that bird, the shortness of whose bill brings the nostril nearly as far forward as in a Goose ; the feet are red or orange, while in the Smew they are grey ; the bulb in the windpipe is larger, and they are very much larger birds.

The Goosander.

Merganser castor, BLANFORD, Faun. Brit. Ind., Birds, Vol. IV, p. 469.

VERNACULAR NAMES.—None in Ind.; in Yarkand *Ala ghaz aurdak* (Pied Goose-duck).

The *male* and *female* differ very much in this species. In the former there is a short, bushy, silky, mane-like crest, while the female's crest is much longer and more straggling ; the shoulder plumes (*scapulars*) and inner quills (*tertials*) in the male are long and pointed, shorter in the female.

In colour the *male* is mostly white, but the head and upper neck are deep green-black, the upper back, scapulars, and narrow edges of tertials are black, the front edge of the wing is black and white, the pinion quills (*primaries*) are greyish-black; the tail and the middle of the lower back are slaty grey, and the sides of the lower back are pencilled with that colour on the white ground. The white lower plumage is sometimes washed with a beautiful salmon-colour, but this is not always present, and disappears in preserved skins.

The *female* is clear slate-grey above, this colour gradually passing into the white of the breast and rest of the underparts; the primary quills are grey-black as in the male, and the quills of the forearm (*secondaries*) and their coverts white, with the exception of the inner ones or tertials, which are grey like the back. The head and neck are chestnut, with the crown greyish brown and the throat white.

The *male* in undress, and the *young*, closely resemble the female; but the young are duller, and the male has a dark ring round the neck, and in undress a darker back and whiter wings. The red of the bill and feet is less bright in the female than in the male, and the feet are orange in the young. The eyes are red in old males, brown in others.

The male is about two feet long, with the wing about eleven inches, the beak about two-and-a-half, and the shank about two; in the female, the wing is about an inch less.

The Goosander inhabits the north temperate region in both hemispheres; in India it breeds, as above stated, in the higher Himalayas, migrating in winter to the base of the range, the hills south of Assam, and the country between the Ganges and Godavari; it has also occurred at Myitkyina in Northern Burma, and is said to have been shot on the east side of Bombay harbour. It is found in pairs in summer in the Himalayas, and in flocks in winter, frequenting rivers and lakes. Young have been taken in the hills in June

(Page 35) H. Grönvold, del.

Smew.

(Page 31) H. Grönvold, del.

Goosander.

and July, but never eggs. The bird breeds either on the ground in long grass or bushes or among stones, or in holes and stumps of trees, most frequently the latter. Mr. Hume thinks it probable they breed in rocks with us. The eggs are buffy-white, and from seven to twelve in number.

The Goosander is very voracious; a captive bird I had under observation devoured no less than forty fish, about two inches long, at a meal. No "castings" were found, but bones and all were digested as by a Cormorant, and the excreta were semi-fluid and very fœtid. The stomach of this bird proved to be soft throughout, not hard and muscular like a Duck's gizzard. The teeth must be very useful in retaining fish, as the bird has no particular power of grip in the bill compared with other fish-eating birds, such as Cormorants.

The Goosander is said to be fair eating if stewed with rich sauce—a thing worth knowing, as it often occurs where no other Duck is found.

The Red-breasted Merganser.

Merganser serrator, BLANFORD, Faun. Brit. Ind., Birds, Vol. IV, p. 470.

VERNACULAR NAMES.—None known.

This Merganser is a smaller bird than the Goosander, but has a longer and narrower bill, with more teeth, and less hooked at the tip. The sexes differ structurally in just the opposite way to those of the other species, the *male* Merganser having a long straggling double crest, consisting of an upper and lower portion, and the *female* a shorter one. The *male* of this species resembles in general the male Goosander in colour and markings, with the following noteworthy differences:—The back is more black, the breast is reddish brown with ill-defined black streaks; the whole front edge of the wing is grey, and there are two black bars across the white part; there is a patch of white black-edged feathers just in front of the armpit; and the lower part of the back is finely pencilled with black and white, this marking being continued more coarsely on the upper flanks.

The *female* is very like the female Goosander, but is of a dull mottled brownish grey instead of the clear pale bluish grey of that bird; the head is not so reddish, and the white of the throat is duller and less clearly defined; and the white patch on the wing formed by the secondaries and their coverts is crossed by a black bar, this occupying the same position as the shorter of the two black wing-bars of the male.

The *young* and the *male in undress* closely resemble the female.

Young birds and females have less bright red feet than males, and there is more black along the ridge of the bill in these; the male has bright red eyes. The male of this species is about twenty-two inches long, with a wing of about nine and three-quarter inches, and shank nearly two; bill about two and-a-half. The female is smaller.

This species of Merganser, like the Goosander, inhabits the north temperate zone of both worlds, breeding in the north and wintering to the southwards. It is a ground breeder, laying eight or more dirty buff eggs. It has only occurred in India twice so far as is known, but probably often gets confused with the Goosander. There are, Dr. Blanford informs us, in the British Museum the wings of one obtained at Karachi by Major Yerbury and in the Indian Museum there was a good skin of a female or young male specimen obtained in the Calcutta bazaar on December 17th, 1889.

The Smew.

Mergus albellus, BLANFORD, Faun. Brit. Ind., Birds, Vol. IV, p. 467.

VERNACULAR NAMES.—*Nihenne*, H., Etawah, N.-W. P.

The *male* Smew is at once distinguished from all other Indian wildfowl by its striking plumage, which is nearly all white. The head, neck, and lower parts are white; but there is a black patch from the bill to behind the eye, and another at the back of the head; the upper back is black, and a black line runs from this at each shoulder down the breast; the scapulars are white with black oblique bars at the tips. The black of the back shades into the grey of the tail-coverts and tail, and the white flanks are pencilled with black. The wings have a black front edge and white "shoulders;" the primaries are brownish black, the secondaries and their coverts black, with white tips forming two bars, and the tertials grey and not very long.

The *female* is dark grey above, this colour extending, mixed with white, across the breast; the head is chestnut with a black patch on the face, and the throat and front of the neck white; the wings are black and white as in the male. The crest is shorter than in that sex.

The *young birds* are like the female, but have no black patch on the face, and the white patch on the wing is clouded with brown; the *male in undress* is also very like the female, but shows the dark bands on the breast. The eyes are brown, but sometimes at all events white in males: the bill and feet are grey, not red as in the other Mergansers. The male is about sixteen inches long, with a wing about eight; bill about one and-a-half, shank one and-a-quarter.

The Smew is confined to the old world, breeding far north, and visiting in winter Central and Southern

Europe, Central Asia, China, and Northern India. With us it is fairly common in the Punjab, and occurs also in Sind, Northern Guzerat, the North-West Provinces, and Oudh. It has also been recorded from Cuttack, and Dr. Blanford has met with it near Raniganj in Bengal, but it has not been observed further east, nor in Southern India.

This is a particularly neat-looking and trimly-built little bird, the most active and vigorous of all our wildfowl. While, as one might expect from its build, a splendid diver, it, as would hardly be guessed from its small wings and large feet, rises readily and flies easily, and gets about nimbly enough on land, where, however, it seems to be very rarely seen in a wild state—I judge from captives in the London Zoo. It builds in holes in trees, laying about half-a-dozen very polished creamy white eggs. It is found in India in flocks, and most of the birds seen there are immature. The flesh is said to be very bad indeed, it being, according to Pallas, "*pisculentissima.*"

The Scaled Merganser.

Merganser squamatus, SALVADORI, Brit. Mus. Cat., Birds, Vol. XXVII, p. 478.

This little-known Chinese species is to some extent intermediate between the GOOSANDER and RED-BREASTED MERGANSER, which it closely resembles in general appearance. The *male*, however, is readily distinguishable from either species by having the black of the head continued down to join that of the upper back, and by the lower black and the flanks being marked with black concentric lines on a white ground, giving a scaly effect. The breast and abdomen are white with a salmon flush in the living bird, as in the Goosander. The crest, however, is double, as in the RED-BREASTED species, and there are also two black bars across the white of the wing.

The *female* is very similar to the female Goosander, but can be recognized by the double crest.

In size this species is very like the Goosander, the male being two feet long, with the bill about two and-a-half inches, shank nearly two, and wing just over ten; the female being smaller.

For many years this MERGANSER, which is found in China, was only known by a young male procured in 1864, but in 1898 an adult pair were procured by Captain Wingate, and figured in the "Ibis" for 1900. These came from South-West HUNAN and since then the species has been found in Yunnan and Western Szechuen, so that it may be expected sooner or later to turn up within Indian limits.

CHAPTER V.

True Ducks.

THERE is no single character marking off this sub-family, which includes the vast majority of species, as there exists in it an infinite variety of form, adapting the birds to various conditions of life; some of the true Ducks being as much land-birds as the Geese, while others are as aquatic as the Mergansers, or even more so. Moreover, the plumage and even size varies immensely according either to species or sex.

The members of this sub-family, however, may nevertheless be easily distinguished from those of the others by negative characters, as pointed out in my introductory chapter. They never have, like Swans, *excessively* long necks, nor equal a tame Goose in size; nor (except in the Golden-eye) are the nostrils ever set as far from the root of the bill as from the tip, as in the Geese; nor do their bills ever show the very narrow form found in the Mergansers, with the tip less than half as broad as the root.

In most cases, however, the bill of a true Duck will at once distinguish it from any member of the family except a Swan, with which there is no danger of any confusion. A Duck's bill is normally broad and shallow, especially towards the tip, of which the nail, as a rule, forms the centre only and is turned down into a more or less marked hook; the nostrils are near the base; and the lower chap is so much smaller than the upper that it shuts quite into it, and cannot be seen from the side, while in most Geese and in Mergansers it is quite visible when the bill is shut. The sides of the bill are parallel, or it enlarges towards the end, tapering in a few cases only, and then not much. The armature of its edges is a sifting apparatus in the form of rows of plates or ridges, the ends of those belonging to the upper chap being sometimes, but rarely, visible when the bill is closed.

All true Ducks have a bill of this type, but of the other sub-families the Mute-Swan and the Bar-headed Goose have a very similar one ; these, however, need no more to be mistaken for Ducks than the latter, when possessed of an eccentric beak, for Swans, Geese or Mergansers.

The males, or drakes, in this sub-family generally possess the bulb or drum at the base of the windpipe alluded to in my account of the Mergansers, and this varies in form according to the genus and species ; the voice of the drake differs accordingly from that of the duck. They are larger than the females, sometimes only a little, but occasionally very much so. They may either resemble them closely in plumage, or differ from them so much as hardly to be recognizable, and there are gradations between these two extremes. As a rule, where the difference exists, the male after breeding assumes a plumage resembling more or less completely that of the female. The young usually resemble her, but may have a special plumage of their own, differing from that of either parent.

In consequence of all these variations, although the drakes in full plumage are remarkably easy to distinguish, it is a matter of some difficulty to find characters which will discriminate every species irrespectively of age, sex, or season. This, however, can be done if attention be paid to details. The fact should be specially noted that in the true Ducks, as in the Mergansers, the secondary quills and their coverts are very commonly so coloured as to produce a wing-bar (*speculum*) or ribbon mark, especially conspicuous when the wing is closed. This is common as a rule to all individuals of the species, though occasionally less developed in females and young.

In habits, as above observed, Ducks vary exceedingly; in addition to their varying attachment to the water, and the corresponding difference in their powers of locomotion there and on land, there is much diversity in their nesting-habits, most breeding on the ground, while some select trees; and these usually perch freely, though from the formation of their feet they cannot move about among the boughs so easily as do most perching birds. Most breed out of India, to the north, but, except the Goosander, all the few resident Indian water fowl belong to this sub-family.

In diet Ducks are omnivorous, though some species are more vegetarian and others more carnivorous than others; grain and shell-fish find especial favour with them. The ridging of the bill enables this organ to be used very effectively for straining small items in their dietary from mud or water. Some feed below the surface, plunging for their food, while others only tilt up their tails and reach down, maintaining their position by padding with the feet.

As there are no less than twenty-nine species in this sub-family, their discrimination is a matter of more difficulty than that of the others. I shall, however, divide them for convenience into manageable groups separated by easily appreciable characters. And in the descriptions of the species I shall avoid as far as possible describing the often complicated colouring of the plumage in too much detail, while laying stress on the salient points of the species.

According to their build and (more or less) corresponding habits, we may divide the true Ducks into diving Ducks, Goose-like Ducks, and ordinary surface-feeding Ducks, groups easily recognizable.

The *diving* Ducks are at once marked off by their large feet, which have the outer toe as long as or even longer than the middle, and the hind toe with a deep lobe or flap, so as to be leaf-like in outline, as in the Mergansers.

All the others have the outer toe markedly shorter than the middle, and the hind toe with a narrow lobe or none at all.

The *goose-like, or walking and perching* Ducks have either a short bill or long shanks, or both, the bill being about the length of the shank; other Ducks have it noticeably longer than the shank.

All of the rest, the *ordinary surface-feeding* Ducks, have rather short shanks and moderate-sized feet, with the outer toe shorter than the middle, and the bill longer than the shank. Most of the species belong to the sub-division of the sub-family.

To take the *diving* Ducks first: in addition to the peculiarity in the formation of their feet, which is manifestly designed to increase the effect of the outward and backward stroke in diving, they are noticeable for their squat form and short necks, wings, legs and tails; the shank is much shorter than the middle toe, and the wings are pointed, and bear a white bar or none at all. They are fine divers, and get their food largely by plunging for it; they do not come ashore much, and walk clumsily, the feet being set far astern. They usually show less difference between the sexes than most surface-feeders do; the bulb in the male's windpipe is partly of bone and partly of membrane. They are often poor eating. They number eight species, divided into four genera, which are very easily distinguished as follows:—

The *Golden-eye* is marked off at once by its forwardly placed nostrils, these being actually nearer to the tip of the bill than to the root.

The *Stiff-tail* by its peculiar wiry tail-feathers, scanty tail-coverts, and very short wings, the primaries not showing when these are closed. The others have ordinary bills and tails, with wings, though small, of reasonable size.

The *Red-crested Pochard* is distinguished by its more or less red or orange feet, while the *ordinary Pochards* (five species) all have grey feet. I shall treat of their distinctions *inter se* when I come to them in their turn.

The Golden-eye.

Clangula glaucion, BLANFORD, Faun. Brit. Ind., Birds, Vol. IV, p. 464.

VERNACULAR NAMES.—*Burgee*, Panjab.

In addition to the peculiarity of its forwardly-placed nostrils, the Golden-eye's bill is remarkable for its shortness and depth at the root; it lowers rapidly to the tip, and the sides also taper somewhat. The wings and tail are rather long for a diving-duck's but narrow; the shanks short, and the feet very large, the middle toe being about twice the length of the shank.

The *male's* plumage is mostly white, but the head is dark glossy green, with a white patch on each side at the base of the beak; the back, edge of the wing, primary and tertiary quills are black; the scapulars are white with black edges, and the tail dark grey or black.

The *female* is dark grey where the male is black, and has a dark brown head with no white on the face, and the white of the wing mixed with dark; the grey of the upper surface extends more or less across the breast. The *young* and the *male in undress* resemble the female, but males are whiter on the wings according to age.

The bill is black in the male, blackish in the female and young, sometimes with a yellow patch at the tip in these latter. The eyes are yellow, and the feet yellow with black webs.

The male is about seventeen inches long, with a bill of about two inches, wing nine and shank one and-a-half. Female considerably smaller.

The Golden-eye inhabits the north temperate and sub-arctic regions of both hemispheres, breeding far north and migrating south in winter ; it is rare in India, but several specimens have been obtained in the Indus Valley, which it apparently visits regularly, and one in Oudh. The Indian Museum also contained a specimen from Sibsaugor, Assam ; and according to a writer in the Rangoon Gazette, November 26th, 1908, it occurs regularly in small flocks on the Irrawaddy.

This species is an active bird, a fine diver and a swift flyer, the wings producing a strong whistling sound in flight. It seldom comes ashore, but can walk well enough. It feeds mostly on animal food, including small fish, and is itself very fishy eating. It breeds in holes of trees and lays about a dozen greyish green eggs. In the structure of its breastbone and windpipe, as well as in plumage and habits, it resembles the Mergansers, and is undoubtedly the nearest ally of that group.

The Stiff-tail.

Erismatura leucocephala, BLANFORD, Faun. Brit. Ind., Birds, Vol. IV, p. 466.

VERNACULAR NAMES.—None known.

This is a most remarkable-looking Duck, *very* short and squat in build, with a broad bill very high and angular at the base, and suddenly sinking towards the end, with the very small nail bent underneath at a sharp angle. The bill is much broader at the end than at the base.

The wing is pointed and absurdly short and small, the primaries not showing when it is closed ; the tail varies in length, but the feathers are noticeably very narrow and stiff, and the tail-coverts, usnally so full in Ducks, short and scanty, giving the tail the appearance of being stuck in. The short legs are set far back, and the feet enormous, the middle toe being fully twice the length of the shank. The plumage is equally characteristic, being finely pencilled above with black on a reddish ground in both sexes, and silvery buff below, the dark bases of the feathers showing. Some specimens are much redder than others.

The *male* has a white head with a black crown, and a blackish neck ; the upper tail-coverts are chestnut.

In the *female* the head is blackish, with the throat and a stripe under the eye white ; the tail-coverts are pencilled like the back. It is apparently about the size of the male.

Young birds resemble the female.

The male's bill is sky-blue, that of the female and young greyish black ; the eyes are dark and the feet grey with black webs.

The length is about fifteen inches, bill about two, shank about one, and wing only about six.

The Stiff-tail is found from the Mediterranean to Central Asia, and is generally resident. Stragglers have occurred from Western Europe to India. It has been found in Kashmir, at Peshawar, near Ludiana, Delhi, and Roorkee, at Mardan, in Gilgit, in the Calcutta bazaar (twice to my knowledge) and near Hardoi. The bird shot in the last locality, by Captain E. D. White, was in full moult in January, and quite unable to fly, so that this species is doubtless resident in India, as the Indian migratory waterfowl are through their moult long before the time. In habits the Stiff-tail resembles a Grebe rather than a Duck. It is more ready to dive

(Page 45) H. Grönvold, del.

Red-crested Pochard.

(Page 42) H. Grönvold, del.

Golden-eye.

than to fly; swims low, with its tail raised, and is said to be unable to walk, but this I doubt, though I have only had a cripple to study; at any rate, the Australian Musk-duck (*Biziura lobata*) which is one of the Stiff-tailed group, walks well enough, but with the gait and semi-erect attitude of a Cormorant. This bird resembled a Grebe in its remarkable tameness and in its constant pluming of its feathers. It builds among reeds or grass, and lays seven to nine eggs, of white colour and remarkably rough coarse surface. The male has no bulb in the windpipe, as was long ago recorded by Pallas.

The Red-crested Pochard.

Netta rufina, BLANFORD, Faun. Brit. Ind., Birds, Vol. IV, p. 456.

VERNACULAR NAMES.—*Lal-chonch*, *Lal-sir*, H.; *Hero-hans* (male), *Chobra-hans* (female), Beng.; *Dumar* (male), *Sanwa* (female), Nepal; *Ratoha*, Sind.

This species differs more from any of the other Pochards than these do from each other, and on that account is placed in a separate genus, though it is far less distinct from them than are the Golden-eye and Stiff-tail, and had better, I think, have been left in the same group. It is the biggest of the Pochards, and further remarkable for its large powerful bill, with the sides tapering or at least parallel, and the ridges lining it few and large, the ends of those belonging to the upper chap showing when the bill is closed. It is more slightly built than Pochards in general, and has the head-feathering thick and full, especially in the male, which is altogether different in plumage from the female. The young resemble her. The red or orange colouring on the bill and feet is characteristic.

The *male* has a full soft bushy crest of a yellow-buff colour, the rest of the head being of a beautiful pinkish chestnut; the upper surface is plain light brown, with two white patches in front of the wings; there is a wing-bar, white in front and pale grey behind, and the pinion-quills are white on the inner edge. The lower surface from the neck is black, as are the rump and shoulders; the sides and wing-lining are white, washed with salmon-pink in birds in fullest plumage.

The bill is pinky scarlet, the eyes red, and the feet orange-red with black webs.

The *female* has less of a crest, and is light brown above and dirty white below from chin to tail. The wings are coloured as in the male, but less purely. The legs are not so bright as in the male, the eyes brown and the bill black, reddish towards the tip. The *young* and the *male in undress* are like her, but the male retains his red bill. I once saw a female in the Calcutta bazaar with a white face like a female Scaup.

The male is about twenty inches long, with an eleven-inch wing, and shank nearly two inches; bill rather over two. The female is smaller.

The Red-crested Pochard breeds in Southern Europe and North Africa, near the Black and Caspian Seas, and in Persia and Eastern Turkestan. It lays about eight eggs of a greenish grey colour. Throughout Northern and Central India it is found in winter, but is rare in the Deccan and further South. It is found in Assam and Manipur, and is believed to occur in Ceylon and in Burma.

It is a good swimmer and diver, has a strong flight, lighter than that of Pochards in general, and it also comes ashore more than other Pochards, walking better on land than these. It is often found in very large flocks on arrival at the beginning of the cold weather, but these afterwards break up into smaller parties. As an article of food it varies, being sometimes good, but often poor eating. Like most other Pochards, it breeds outside India, and its note is a deep grating *kurr*, rather a croak than a quack. The male has the bulb of the windpipe partly of bone and partly of membrane ; he sometimes whistles, this sound being apparently not made by the female.

The other five Pochards (genus *Nyroca*) form a very recognizable and uniform group. They all have grey and black bills and feet, and are clumsily formed, with large close-feathered heads. Except the Common or Red-headed Pochard, all have a white wing-bar formed by the secondary quills, and the inner primaries at least mostly white internally. The males, from their few and striking colours, are remarkably easy to distinguish, but the females are more alike, though less so than is usual in surface feeders. The young so resemble each other that their discrimination is the only real difficulty in the study of our Indian Ducks ; they have generally a distinct plumage of their own in this stage. The male's *undress* does not differ so much from his ordinary garb as is usual in Ducks.

All of them have bills which broaden more or less towards the end ; and the male's windpipe has a drum partly of bone and partly of membrane. The note is a harsh croak, like "*kurr*," and is seldom heard. They are all excellent divers, feeding under water, difficult to retrieve if only wounded, and more or less clumsy on land, where they seldom venture. Their flight is laboured, and they rise with difficulty as a rule.

Independently of age and sex, they may be distinguished as follows :—

The *Red-headed Pochard* has no white bar on the wing as above stated.

The *Tufted Pochard* usually has a narrow crest, of varying length according to age and sex.

The *Scaup* has a bill very broad towards the tip, its width at the widest part being more than equal to the distance between the front edge of the nostril and the nail, while in the others (except the Tufted, whose crest and smaller size distinguish it) it is less.

The Common and *Eastern White-eyes* have no crest and an ordinary-shaped bill ; they are distinguished by the colour of the crown, the Eastern White-eye having this dark green or blackish, while it is plain or red-brown in the other, which is also smaller.

The Red-headed Pochard.

Nyroca ferina, BLANFORD, Faun. Brit. Ind., Birds, Vol. IV, p. 458.

VERNACULAR NAMES.—*Burar-nar*, *Lal-sir*, H.; *Lal muriya*, Beng.; *Cheun*, Nepal ; *Thording-nam*, Manipur.

This is a very ungainly looking Duck. The bill is long and rather narrow, the head and feet very large, and the tail and wings short.

The *male* is at once known from any Indian Duck by his conspicuous tri-coloured plumage, the head being rich chestnut red, the breast, rump, and stern black, and the body pale clear grey, this colour being produced by a fine pencilling of black (grey on the wings), the white prevailing below.

The *female* (sometimes called the Dunbird) has a nut-brown head and breast, shaded with white about the cheeks and throat, a dark dirty grey body, the pencilling less marked and on a darker ground, and replaced by dark and light mottling below, and tail-coverts not so black as in the male. Both have a plain inconspicuous grey wing-bar. The *young* appear to resemble the female, but are browner, at any rate below, and the *male in undress* retains much of his full colour, merely getting

(Page 51) H. Grönvold, del.

Tufted Pochard.

(Page 48) H. Grönvold, del.

Red-headed Pochard.

a browner head, a dark pencilled grey breast and duller tail-coverts.

The male has bright red or, rarely, yellow eyes ; the female, usually, at all events, brown ones ; the bill and feet are grey and black, *as in all Pochards of this genus*, lightest and brightest in old males.

The male is about seventeen inches long, with a wing of about eight and-a-half inches, shank an inch and-a-half, and bill just over two. The female is smaller.

This Pochard inhabits the whole north temperate zone in the Old World, breeding to the north, and migrating southward in winter, when it visits Northern India in large numbers ; further south it is less common, but occurs as far as Bellary. It has not yet been obtained in Mysore or farther south, nor in Ceylon, but is not uncommon in Assam and Manipur, and has been recorded from the neighbourhood of Mandalay.

This Pochard swims particularly low in the water, and very much down by the stern ; it looks ungainly in the extreme on land, but walks well enough when there ; it seems to rise on the wing with considerable difficulty. Like all Pochards, it is a ground breeder ; its greenish-grey eggs may number as many as twelve. A male's eyes have been observed to change colour from red to yellow when it was handled. It usually occurs in India in large flocks, frequenting especially large tanks or jheels, but also the sea-coast. Away from this, it is one of the best Ducks for the table, and might well be called the Indian Canvas-back, since the celebrated American Duck of that name so closely resembles it that an unfortunate poulterer in England who had received Canvas-backs from America in ice was actually prosecuted for selling Pochards in close time ! The Canvas-back (*Nyroca vallisneria*) is, however, very much bigger than our Pochard, darker on the head and lighter below, and with an entirely

4

black bill. Another Pochard also occurs in America still more like our bird (*N. americana*) ; this has yellow eyes and less black on the bill.

The Scaup.

Nyroca marila, BLANFORD, Faun. Brit. Ind., Birds, Vol. IV, p. 462.

VERNACULAR NAMES.—None known.

This species is very like the Red-headed Pochard in size and general pattern of colour, but has a shorter and very much broader bill, this being much wider at the tip than at the base.

The *male* has a deep black-green head, and a black breast, rump, and stern ; the body is coarsely pencilled black and white, and the quills black with a white bar on the secondaries and white shading on the inner primaries ; the belly is white.

The *female* has a brown head and breast, the latter gradually passing into the white of the belly ; there is a white band round the root of the bill ; the pattern of colour generally is the same as the male but with brown instead of black ; the *male in undress* has a similar plumage.

The *young* are of a general dirty brown colour with a white face as in females, and with brown and white wings like theirs ; the belly is also white. The eyes are always yellow in this species, apparently, certainly in males.

The Scaup inhabits the whole of the north temperate zone, breeding to the north and going south in winter. It lays eight or nine dirty buff eggs. It is chiefly, in Europe at all events, a salt-water bird, and it is probably for this reason that it has been very rarely recorded from India. But it has occurred in Kashmir,

Kulu, Nepal, the neighbourhood of Attock, Gurgaon near Delhi, Karachi, and Bombay.

The Tufted Pochard.

Nyroca fuligula, BLANFORD, Faun. Brit. Ind., Birds, Vol. IV, p. 463.

VERNACULAR NAMES.—*Dubaru*, *Ablak*, *Rohwora*, H.; *Turando*, Sind; *Malac*, Nepal Terai; *Nella Chilluwa*, Tel.; *Neer bathoo*, Tamil; *Neer-kolee*, Canarese.

This is, if not a graceful, a neat-looking little Duck, with a short bill, much broadened towards the tip as in the Scaup, and a very compact "tubby" form; the head has a narrow crest, small in females and very small in young, but long and tassel-like in full plumaged males, in which it hangs far down. The *male* is easily distinguished by his black and white colouration, nearly the whole plumage being black, but the belly and sides are pure white, there being also the usual white on the quills. The inner quills are glossed with green, and the head with purple. In *undress* the crest is shorter and the flanks clouded with a black pencilling.

The *female* has the same distribution of colour, but the white is not so extensive or so clearly defined, and the black is replaced by more or less deep brown, the lightest birds having least white on the flanks, which may be entirely dirty brown. The difference probably depends on age. Some females have white on the fore-part of face, much as in the female Scaup.

The *young bird* has a general dirty light brown colour with dark-brown wings marked with white as in the parents.

The eyes are yellow in this species; rich orange yellow in old males, paler in females and young, in which latter they may even be white or brown. Hence this bird is sometimes, but incorrectly, called the Golden-eye, this name being used and wanted for the very different species described above.

The bill is nearly all of a blue-grey colour, only the tip being black, and is much brighter in the old males than in others.

The length is about eighteen inches, the wing eight inches, the shank one and-a-half, and the bill just under two.

The female is a little smaller.

The Tufted Pochard inhabits the northern part of the Old World, breeding in the north and migrating south in winter as far as Abyssinia, China and India, and straying even to the Malay Peninsula and Polynesia. It is suspected of breeding in the hills in Abyssinia and may do so in India. It is rather a late breeder, laying in June ; the eggs number eight and are pale olive green. As it has bred and multiplied most freely on the London park waters, and numbers fly about there unpinioned, it would be a good idea to introduce it on lakes in Indian hill stations. In India it is common in the Deccan, Central Provinces, and Chota Nagpur ; it is also found in the Indo-Gangetic plain, but not abundantly. It does not appear to go further south in India than the northern part of the Coimbatore district. In Manipur it has been found very abundant, and has also been met with near Mandalay.

It commonly occurs singly or in small flocks, but sometimes in large numbers, and frequents open sheets of water ; it is a very fine diver. On land it moves more awkwardly than any Pochard I know, hobbling as if lame in both feet. It is partial to animal food, and said to be not first-class for eating. It breeds more freely in captivity than do Pochards in general, and in the London Zoological Gardens in 1849 crossed with the White-eye, the resulting hybrids continuing to breed either *inter se* or with the original parents for more than ten years—a fact to be remembered in dealing with doubtful Pochards, which should therefore whenever possible be submitted to some authority for identification.

The Green-headed Pochard or Baer's White-eye.

Nyroca bæri, BLANFORD, Faun. Brit. Ind., Birds, Vol. IV, p. 461.

VERNACULAR NAMES.—*Boro Lalbigra*, Cachar.

This Duck is somewhat slighter and less squatty in build than Pochards generally, being distinguishable in this respect even from its near ally the common White-eye.

The *male* has a dark glossy green head and neck and a glossy deep bay or chocolate breast; the upper plumage and wings are deep glossy brown, with the usual white on the quills; the under surface from the breast is white, and this extends halfway up the flanks, but above passes gradually into light-brown. The eyes are white, or very rarely, yellow.

The *female* is like the male, but has a rust-coloured patch on each side of the face at the root of the beak; the green of the head is less bright and is mixed slightly with rusty about the throat; the breast is lighter, nor is its colour so sharply defined from the white belly as in the male, and there is less white on the flanks. The *male in undress* assumes the rusty facial patch, and gets some white mottling on the breast, and the white appears to fade at this time off the flanks of both sexes.

The eyes of the female are brown, rarely grey or whitish.

The *young birds* are of a dirty light-brown, with wings and tail much as in the parents. The crown is blackish, and there is a rusty patch on the face as in the old female. The colour of the eyes is already quite different in the sexes even in this plumage, so it must develop early.

The length of the male of this species is about nineteen inches ; the wing about eight inches ; the shank about an inch and-a-half, and the bill two inches ; the female is smaller than the male, especially as regards the bill. But females in this species appear to vary in size much more than males, and, as in the Tufted Pochard, some are much duller and less like the males than are others.

This Pochard inhabits Eastern Siberia, China, and Japan normally, but appears to be a bird of somewhat erratic habits. Even in China it is not always to be found easily, and to India it is certainly, I think, a most irregular visitor, though it has probably often been passed over for the White-eye, to which bird the young certainly bear a very close resemblance, though the old birds are easily distinguishable. It was apparently obtained from Bengal in 1825, and Blyth certainly got one female in the Calcutta bazaar in 1842 or 1843, but did not identify it, which is not surprising, seeing that this Duck had not then been recognized as a distinct species. Then, at the end of February 1896, I got eleven full-plumaged birds there, and after that the species came for a time in greater or less numbers every winter, being very common in 1896-97 and less so in 1897-98. I got three males and a female in February 1899, and saw what was either a small dull female or a hybrid with the common White-eye about the middle of January. We had in the Indian Museum other birds in plumage intermediate between the two White-eyes, and I therefore think that they inter-breed. In the cold weather of 1899-1900, I did not see more than half-a-dozen specimens, but 1901 I again saw a few. In 1902, however, none appeared in the market.

The wild habits of this Duck are said to resemble those of the Common White-eye, next to be noticed, and it lays similar eggs ; my own observations on its ways have been restricted to captives. It is a better walker than most Pochards, and, I have fancied, hardly so fine a diver. It certainly, judging from birds in the fine water aviary in the Alipore Zoological Gardens, rises more easily on the wing and flies with less effort than other Pochards. I noticed that at Alipore our birds could rise well up into the roof and fly round and round like the surface-feeding Ducks. In captivity in India the species appears to stand the heat less well than the common White-eye. I am ashamed to say, having had more to do with this species than probably any one, that I do not know how it tastes! But Mr. E. C. Stuart Baker, who does, pronounces it very bad.

The White-eye.

Nyroca ferruginea, BLANFORD, Faun. Brit. Ind., Birds, Vol. IV, p. 460.

VERNACULAR NAMES.—*Karchiya*, *Burar-mada*, H.; *Lalbigri*, *Bhuti-hans*, Beng.; *Burnu*, Sind; *Malac*, Nepal Terai.

This species, sometimes, but very erroneously, called a "Wigeon" by sportsmen, is the smallest of all our Pochards, being slighter, if not much shorter, than the Tufted species.

The *male* has the head, breast, and flanks, rich glossy bay or mahogany-red ; the belly and stern are white, and the upper plumage and wings dark brown, with the usual white on the latter, and the inner quills glossed green. It appears not to go into *undress* at all. The eyes are white, this colour appearing before the bird is in full plumage.

The *female* is much duller and darker in colour, has not the white belly so clearly defined from the breast, and has grey eyes, but is otherwise similar.

The *young bird* is of a general dirty yellowish brown, with wings and tail as in the old. It is rather reddish about the head generally, but shows no black shade on the crown, and by this and its smaller size can be distinguished from the young of the Eastern White-eye. The old birds on the water are easily distinguishable at a distance, not only by the size, but by the present species showing no white above the water-line except on the stern.

The male is about seventeen inches long, with a wing about seven, shank rather over one, and bill about one-and-three quarters. The females are smaller.

This little Pochard inhabits the Mediterranean area, Central and Eastern Europe, and South-Western Asia, having thus a more southerly range than most Pochards. It is resident, and breeds in Kashmir, and in winter visits the plains of India, being common throughout Northern India, as far East as Bengal; in Northern Burma, Assam, and Manipur, whence I have examined a pair, procured by Lieutenant H. H. Turner, and now in the Indian Museum. In Central India, the Central Provinces, and the Bombay Presidency, it is less abundant, but no rarity; but it occurs only occasionally about Ratnagiri and has not yet been recorded from Southern India or Ceylon.

This White-eye likes weedy waters, and does not associate in large flocks, rising, when disturbed, in twos or threes. It is a splendid diver, and owing to the localities it frequents, peculiarly difficult to capture if only winged. I do not think, however, it dives so well as the Tufted and Common Pochards. Before leaving India I had my water-fowl caught up from the Indian Museum

(Page 65) H. Grönvold, del.

Small Whistler.

(Page 55) H. Grönvold, del.

White-eyed Pochard.

tank by native fishermen with nets, and though the White-eyes of both species [this and *N. bæri*] were readily captured, I had to abandon the attempt to net the others mentioned. It breeds in the Kashmir lakes in June, laying nine or ten buff-coloured eggs in a nest made of dry rushes placed amid thick reeds, etc., close to the water. It is said to be very poor eating, but I have found it palatable enough ; it was commonly eaten in Calcutta in my time.

There are a number of other Asiatic diving-ducks, which, being mostly marine, except in the breeding-season, are not likely to occur in India, but may be expected to turn up on the Chinese Coast. They all present the typical diving-duck structure in a high degree of development, are mainly animal feeders, and none are very good to eat.

The Long-tailed Duck.

Harelda glacialis, SALVADORI, Brit. Mus. Cat., Birds, Vol. XXVII, p. 389.

This is a rather small, but very distinct-looking Duck, with a very short bill, shorter than the shank, and the tail, in the male, with two long centre-feathers like the Pintail drake's ; this peculiar type of tail only occurs in these two very dissimilar Ducks. The Long-tailed drake, however, retains his long tail-feathers always, even when in undress plumage.

In his full plumage the male is mostly white, but has most of the wings, back, lower breast, and long centre-tail-feathers black ; the head is greyish, and there is a brown patch on the sides of the neck. The male in *summer undress* is mainly black, with the under-parts white, the back variegated by chestnut edgings to the feathers, and the face smoky grey.

The bill is slate-colour with a broad band of salmon-colour, the legs grey, and the eyes reddish-brown.

The *female* has an ordinary short tail, and is dull blackish above, with lighter edgings on the shoulders, and white below ; she also has the sides of the head dirty white, and the throat and neck brown.

The male is about twenty-two inches long, the long centre-tail-feathers accounting for eight, with a bill just over the inch, and shank about an inch and-a-half ; the closed wing is nine inches. The female, though little smaller, is, of course, much shorter on account of the different tail. This handsome Duck is as distinct in habits as in appearance. It is an Arctic bird, ranging all round the northernmost parts of the Northern Hemisphere, and migrating south in winter as far as Italy on the one side and South Carolina on the other. It is found in China and Japan at this season. In its winter haunts it is mainly a sea-duck, and the most oceanic of all, feeding in mid-water on small crustacea, etc., so that it is independent of the bottom. It is a fine diver, and, unlike most diving-ducks, lively and active on the wing, and ready to take flight. The call is a loud gabbling note and often uttered: in fact, the birds are so noisy that they are ungallantly called "Old-Squaw" in America. They breed in high latitudes, laying, about midsummer, half-a-dozen or more greyish-buff eggs in a nest on the ground.

The Harlequin Duck.

Cosmonetta histrionica, SALVADORI, Brit. Mus. Cat., Birds, Vol. XXVII, p. 395.

Shinori-gamo, Japanese.

The Harlequin is another rather small Duck of striking appearance with a short bill about the length of the shank. The tail is of rather more than ordinary length, and pointed, but not excessively long.

The *male* is mostly of a curious dark slaty-blue colour, more what one would expect in a pigeon than a duck, with the wings back and tail black, and flanks chestnut; there is also a streak of chestnut along the head from each eye, and the plumage is curiously diversified by white markings—a stripe along each side of the crown, a patch in front of the eyes and one over each ear, a stripe down the side of the neck, a bar across the neck at the lower part, and another in front of the wing, and sundry markings on the shoulders, and inner wing-feathers. The bill is slate-coloured and the legs brown; the eyes dark.

The *female* is drab above, getting paler on the underparts, with a dirty white forehead and a white patch before the eye, and spot on the ear, as in the drake; the underparts are also marked with white.

The male is about seventeen inches long, with the bill and shank rather over an inch, and the closed wing eight inches.

The distribution of this Duck is curious; it inhabits Greenland and Iceland, but is rare in Europe; it is at home in the Far East of Northern Asia and visits Japan in winter; it also breeds in the North of the New World, going as far as California on migration. It lays eight or more eggs about midsummer, of a creamy colour and smooth surface. It is remarkable for its power of swimming in swift streams, but frequents the sea in winter.

The Scoters (*Oedemia*) are large diving-ducks with good-sized bills, black plumaged in the male and sooty-brown in the female sex, breeding inland in the north, and frequenting the sea in winter. They build on the ground and lay cream-coloured eggs. None occur in India, but some may be looked for on the Chinese coast.

The Common Scoter.

Oedemia nigra, SALVADORI, Brit. Mus. Cat., Birds, Vol. XXVII, p. 401.

Is black all over in the *male*, with the black bill, which has a knob at the base, marked with a broad bright yellow streak down the centre; the legs are dark-olive. The *female* is dark-brown with some white on the throat and abdomen, a black bill and olive legs, the eyes are dark in both. The male is about twenty inches long, with bill about two and-a-half, shank nearly two, and closed wing nine and-a-half.

The common Scoter ranges from Iceland through Lapland, east to the Taimyr Peninsula, and winters as far south as the Mediterranean; it is not a very likely bird to occur in Eastern Asia, where its place is taken by the following species:—

The American Scoter.

Oedemia americana, SALVADORI, Brit. Mus. Cat., Birds, Vol. XXVII, p. 404.

This is very similar to the last, but has the knob on the male's bill all yellow, as is the upper bill generally, but with a scarlet flush along the sides. Although chiefly an American bird, it is found in North-East Asia, and visits Corea and Japan in winter.

The Velvet Scoter.

Oedemia fusca, SALVADORI, Brit. Mus. Cat., Birds, Vol. XXVII, p. 406.

Is a considerably bigger bird than the last two, with the dark plumage diversified by a white wing-bar in both sexes. The black male has his bill, which is swollen at the base, black there and round the edge, orange-yellow elsewhere, and his legs red. He has also a small white patch under the eye. The dark-brown *female* has a large dirty white patch before the eye and a small one behind it; her bill is dark slate-colour.

The male is about twenty-two inches long, with a bill rather over two and-a-half, shank just under two, and wing rather over ten and-a-half.

This Scoter inhabits the northern parts of the Old World generally, migrating south in winter—unless, indeed, records from Eastern Asia concern the next species.

The Eastern Velvet Scoter.

Oedemia carbo, SALVADORI, Brit. Mus. Cat., Birds, Vol. XXVII, p. 411.

In this species the male's bill has a more definite knob at the base and is red at the sides, and the white eye-spot is situated further back. It is the characteristic white-wing-barred Scoter of North-Eastern Asia, and is found in winter on the coasts of Japan and China.

The Surf Scoter.

Oedemia perspicillata, SALVADORI, Brit. Mus. Cat., Birds, Vol. XXVII, p. 412.

Is all black in the *male*, except for a white patch on the crown and another on the back of the neck; the bill is high and swollen all along, unlike that of any other Duck, and is gaily coloured with scarlet, yellow, white and black. The legs are red and the eyes white. The dark-brown female is marked with white on the back of the neck, the throat, and the face; her bill is dark slate, and less exaggerated in form than the male's.

The male is about twenty-one inches long, with the great bill two and-a-half, shank about two, and closed wing nine and-a-half.

This Scoter is an Arctic American bird, but also occurs in the East Asiatic coasts at times.

The Eiders are also northern diving-ducks, especially marine in habits. They breed in the high north on the ground, laying eggs of an olive or greenish drab colour. The males are chiefly black-and-white, and their females mottled-brown, more like those of the surface-feeding Ducks, to which, rather than to the other diving-ducks, they are allied.

The Common Eider.

Somateria mollissima, SALVADORI, Brit. Mus. Cat., Birds, Vol. XXVII, p. 425.

This Eider has a large strong bill, with the feathering of the face running down it, both from the forehead and on the sides from the cheeks. The male is chiefly white above, black on the wings and below, with a black cap and a patch of light green at the back of the head. His bill and feet are olive-green, and eyes dark. In undress he is nearly all black.

The *female* is mottled-brown, sometimes with a black wing-bar bordered with white. The male is about two feet long, with a bill about two inches long, shank rather less, and closed wing nearly a foot. It is a large, heavy-looking Duck.

This bird, the celebrated producer of the Eider-down of commerce—or at least some of it—ranges from Iceland east to the Yenisei, and ranges south in winter to the Mediterranean ; it is practically purely a sea-duck. It is replaced in America by a very nearly-allied race (*S. dresseri*).

The Pacific Eider.

Somateria V-nigrum, SALVADORI, Brit. Mus. Cat., Birds, Vol. XXVII, p. 430.

Has an orange bill in the male, which also possesses a black V-shaped mark on the throat. It inhabits the northern coasts of the Pacific, and when breeding does not keep so close to the sea as the common Eider. It is this species which may be expected to occur on the Chinese coast in winter.

The King Eider.

Somateria spectabilis, SALVADORI, Brit. Mus. Cat., Birds, Vol. XXVII, p. 432.

In this species the *male* has a large knob on the forehead ; his plumage is mostly white above and black below as in the Common and Pacific Eiders, but the cap is lavender-grey. The bill is red, orange on the basal knob, and the legs orange-red.

The *female* is like the common Eider female, but has the feathering of the forehead running down further than in that bird, reaching the level of the nostrils, whereas in the common Eider female it does not come more than half-way. Beside, the present species is a smaller bird, with the male's bill only a little over two, the shank less than two, and the wing hardly over ten inches. This is purely an Arctic Duck, found all round the world, but it has occurred in winter as far south as Venice, and may turn up in China.

The Spectacled Eider.

Arctonetta fischeri, SALVADORI, Brit. Mus. Cat., Birds, Vol. XXVII, p. 422.

In the male of this curious Duck the plumage is mostly white above and dark-grey below, with the back of the head olive-green, but the most characteristic point is a satiny white patch, bordered with black, round the eyes, which is white; the bill is orange and the feet olive. The female is mottled-brown with a bluish bill.

The male measures about twenty-one inches, with the bill an inch long and the shank about one and-a-half; the wing is ten inches. This Duck inhabits the North Pacific, on both sides, but is best known as an American bird.

Steller's Eider.

Heniconetta stelleri, SALVADORI, Brit. Mus. Cat., Birds, Vol. XXVII, p. 419.

This is the smallest of the Eiders, with none of their characteristic peculiarities of bill or face, but very beautiful plumage in the male, which has long hanging shoulder-plumes, of a deep blue with white edgings. The general colouration is complicated and difficult to describe; the head is white, varied with olive-green and blue-black; there is a white patch on the wing, and a purple bar following it; the back is blue-black, and the under parts chestnut. The bill is gray and the feet brown, the eyes dark. The female is of a mottled-brown, with a purplish-black bar, bordered with white, on the wing.

The male is only about eighteen inches long, with the bill just under two inches, and the shank little over one; the wing measures about eight and-a-half.

Steller's Eider inhabits the high northern latitudes of both worlds, but is rare in the west of the Old World; it may perhaps be found to occur on the Chinese coast in winter.

CHAPTER VI.

True Ducks.—(*Continued.*)

HAVING now disposed of the diving *Anatinæ*, we come to the pedestrian and perching contingent, characterized by bearing some resemblance, either in structure or habits, to the Geese, as the divers did to the Mergansers. I group together the genera composing this section purely for convenience, as they have often little in common and are not always nearly related. But the same may be said of some of the diving genera,* which are nevertheless always grouped together; and it is important to break up this big sub-family into manageable groups.

The goose-like Ducks, then, have this common point of difference from the rest of the sub-family, that the bill and shank are about equally long; the latter may be short, and in that case the bill is so also. The bill is never *long*, but a comparatively short bill means a long shank for a Duck if the lengths are equal, an ordinary Duck's beak much exceeding its leg in length. Most of the present section have the sexes alike, or nearly so, in plumage, which is striking, and forms an easy means of identification.

The seven goose-like genera, comprising eight species,

---

* I pointed out above, for instance, that the Golden-eye is nearer the Mergansers than the Pochards; and the Stiff-tail with its foreign allies (genus *Erismatura*) do not closely resemble any other diving Duck, while in plumage at any rate they approach a surface-feeding Duck found in South America (*Heteronetta atricapilla*). The general resemblance in form of diving Ducks goes, no doubt, with the habit of diving—a habit which may be acquired, as I shall later have occasion to mention, by the surface-feeders. The Whistlers are also almost as much divers as Pochards are.

are easily distinguishable from each other and *from all other Indian Ducks* as follows :—

The *Whistlers* (two species) by their short-quilled wings, which are all black beneath.

The *Sheldrake* by its brilliant pied plumage of white, black and chestnut.

The *Brahminy Duck* by its chestnut or buff plumage and black-and-white wings.

The *Comb-duck* by its long dark wings, and white belly.

The *Cotton-teal* by its minute size (smaller than a pigeon) and inch-long bill.

The *Mandarin Duck* by the primary-quills being silvery-grey on the outer and steel blue on the inner web.

The *Wigeon* by the combination of a bill less than two inches long with a ten-inch wing. All Ducks with a bill as short as this have a much shorter wing, not over eight inches. Besides, the blue-grey colour of the Wigeon's bill distinguishes it from all other short-billed species.

The two Whistlers, so-called from their whistling note, belong to a very natural and easily recognizable genus; in addition to the colour of the under-surface of their wings, they are noticeable for the peculiar broad rounded form of these. Though large for the size of the bird, the wings have the pinion-quills very short, not showing when they are folded. The body is of unusual form for a Duck, being light and slim, with the thighs prominent; the legs are set far back, but close together, so that the birds walk without any of the usual swaying or waddling in the gait so proverbially characteristic of Ducks. The neck and shanks are long and the feet large, the middle toe being longer than the shank; the outer toe, however, does not nearly equal it in length, and the hind toe, which is unlobed, is longer than in other Ducks. The tail is very short and rounded, and the body short and narrow;

(Page 88) H. Grönvold, del.

Shoveller.

(Page 78) H. Grönvold, del.

Wigeon.

the bill presents no remarkable point. These birds, as above stated, walk well, though they do not come ashore much. Their flight is easier than that of most Ducks, but not swift or powerful ; they perch freely, and dive for food like Pochards, but with more of a spring. They are omnivorous feeders, fair eating themselves, and build usually in trees. The sexes are alike in plumage, and the young differ very little from them. The two species, though much alike, are easily to be distinguished, as the descriptions will show, so that a key is unnecessary in this case.

The Small Whistler.

Dendrocycga javanica, BLANFORD, Faun. Brit. Ind., Birds, Vol. IV, p. 430.

VERNACULAR NAMES :—*Silli*, *Silhahi*, *Chiheè*, H. *Saral*, *Shareil*, *Harrali-hans*, Beng. ; *Hansrali* Uriya ; *Ade*, *Adla*, Mahrathi ; *Horali*, Assam ; *Tingi*, Manipur ; *Yerra Chilluwa*, Tel. ; *Yerrundi*, Mal. ; *Chemba Tara*, Tam. (Ceylon) ; *Saaru*, *Tatta Saaru*, Cing. ; *Si-sa-li*, Burmese.

This is, in spite of its somewhat awkward proportions, a neat-looking little Duck, with the head, neck, breast and flanks dun ; crown of head brown, belly chestnut, and upper surface slate with chestnut bars. There is a *maroon patch at the root of the tail above*, and the wings are maroon and greyish black above.

Young birds, are altogether dun below, with none of the chestnut colour.

The bill is dark-grey and black, eyellds bright yellow, eyes dark and feet dark-grey.

The length is about a foot and-a-half, the wing between seven and eight inches, and the bill and shank nearly two.

The Small Whistler is a common species almost throughout India, Ceylon, and Burma ; it is found also in the Andaman and Nicobar Islands, and from the Malay Peninsula to Java. In the Himalayas and Panjab, however, it is not found, or only rarely, and is, of course, absent from desert tracts. It is resident, but moves about considerably at different seasons. It frequents wooded localities, perching much on trees, and prefers weedy ponds and marshes to open water. It generally builds on trees, either making a stick nest for itself, or appropriating the deserted home of some other bird ; but it may build in herbage by the water. In most parts of India the breeding season is July and August, but in Ceylon may be as early as February. About a dozen white eggs are laid, and the young, if the nest is high up, are carried down in the feet of the parents. The flesh is said to be poor, but makes good soup. This Duck should not be allowed always to go unscathed by people who despise it as game, for natives are glad to eat it, and it is so quarrelsome with other Ducks that I have no doubt it tends to drive away more valuable species.

The Large Whistler.

Dendrocycga fulva, BLANFORD, Faun. Brit. Ind., Birds, Vol. IV, p. 432.

VERNACULAR NAMES :—*Burra Silli*, H.

This is a considerably bigger bird than the last, and of very ungainly appearance, owing to its large coarse head and bill and very big feet ; the general body colour is chestnut throughout, not on the belly only ; the upper surface is black with chestnut bars, the wings black, with a dark maroon patch, and *a cream-coloured patch replaces the maroon at the root of the tail.* There is a bold black streak down the back of the neck, a whitish shade round the middle of it, and some white dashes on the flanks, in this species.

The bill is grey and black, eyelids French-grey, eyes dark, and feet French-grey, or at any rate much paler than in the Small Whistler.

The Large Whistler is about twenty inches long, with a wing about eight and-a-half, and bill and shank about two and-a-quarter.

It has a very remarkable distribution, being found in Africa south of the Sahara and Madagascar, and in Central and South America, as well as in India south of the Himalayas, Ceylon, Pegu and Toungoo. In the Madras Presidency and the Deccan it is very rare, and fairly common in Lower Bengal ; but over India generally it is scarce. Its rarity may be due to the abundance in India of the Small Whistler, which, I have observed it usually fears and gives way to. It has a stronger and more rapid flight than its relative, is said to be better eating, and occurs in small flocks. It builds in trees ; the eggs are larger than those of the small species.

The Wandering Whistler.

Dendrocycga arcuata, SALVADORI, Brit. Mus. Cat., Birds, Vol. XXVII, p. 153.

Is to a great extent intermediate in size and plumage between our two Indian species. The head has a distinct dark cap, reaching down to the eyes and continued as a black streak down the back of the neck ; the rest of the head and neck are dun, passing into rich bay on the underparts and flanks, which latter are bordered by splashes of cream-colour forming a line along each side, and there is a patch of cream colour on each side on the upper tail-coverts. The back is black with chestnut edgings to the feathers, and the wings black with a maroon patch on the " shoulder ; " but the most readily noticeable point is that the breast is spotted, though somewhat indistinctly, with black. The bill is jet-black, eyes dark, and feet dark slate-colour.

The length of this Duck is about seventeen inches, with the bill and shank nearly two, and closed wing eight and-a-half.

It has a very wide distribution in the East Indies and reaches the Islands of the Pacific, ranging from Java through the Islands to the Australia and even Fiji. In Australia it nests on the ground among grass—laying about a dozen creamy-buff eggs—and is found feeding out on plains at night. Some in confinement in the London Zoo much resemble the Indian Whistlers in their note, sociable habits, and diving for food.

The Spotted Whistler.

Dendrocycga guttata, SALVADORI, Brit. Mus. Cat., Birds, Vol. XXVII, p. 184.

Is about the same size as the last species, but very differently coloured. The general hue above is brown, with lighter edges to the black feathers; the wings are brown, not black; the face and upper neck are greyish and finely pencilled, and the breast and flanks are spotted with white, the abdomen being nearly all white. The bill is black and the feet grey; the eyes brown.

This Duck is an East-Indian species, ranging from Mindanao in the Philippines through Celebes and the Moluccas to New Guinea.

The Sheldrake and Brahminy, though differing so strikingly in plumage, ought certainly to be kept in the same genus, as they are by some ornithologists. Even as to colour, their *wings* are almost identical, being white with black primaries, bronze-green secondaries, and chestnut tertiaries. The different species of Sheldrake (genera *Casarca* and *Tadorna*) are, indeed, so nearly related that they have been known to "throw back" when crossed, like domestic breeds of one species. In the London Zoological Gardens, in 1859, a female of the grey-headed South African Brahminy (*Casarca cana*) very like our bird, crossed with a male of the common Sheldrake (*Tadorna cornuta*), and the result was a couple of pencilled dark-grey birds, very closely resembling the Australian Grey Sheldrake (*Casarca tadornoides*). This reminds one forcibly of the case communicated to Darwin by Brent, wherein a cross between a white *Aylesbury* and a black *Labrador* Duck produced some birds resembling the wild Mallard, the ancestor of both!

Both Sheldrake and Brahminy are noticeable among

our Ducks for their graceful build, with long shanks and wings, nearly square tail and light body. They swim high in the water, and walk and run quickly and gracefully, the legs being set well forward. They are largely land feeders, omnivorous in diet, and build in holes. They are courageous and intelligent, and inclined to associate in pairs rather than in flocks. They are migrants, but the Brahminy builds in our limits in the Himalayas. The sexes are very similar in plumage, and the young closely resemble them.

The Brahminy Duck or Ruddy Sheldrake.

Casarca rutila, BLANFORD, Faun. Brit. Ind., Birds, Vol. IV, p. 428.

VERNACULAR NAMES :—*Chakwa* (male), *Chakwi* (female) ; *Surkhab*, *Lal*, H. ; *Mungh*, Sind ; *Bugri*, Beng. ; *Sarza*, *Chakrawak*, Mahr. ; *Bassana Chituwa*, Tel. ; *Kesar-pandia*, *Pandahansa*, Uriya ; *Nir-bathoo*, *Nir-koli*, South India ; *Hintha*, Burmese.

The Brahminy has an ordinary-shaped, rather short bill. The general colour of the plumage is rich chestnut, varying from this to buff occasionally ; the wings are white, black and bronze-green, as above described ; the rump and tail black, and the head and neck buff. The *male* has in summer a black ring at the base of the buff neck, and the *female* has the fore part of the head white ; otherwise they are alike. The bill, eyes, and feet are all dark.

The male Brahminy is about two feet long, with a fifteen-inch wing, and shank and bill about two and-a-half. The female is smaller.

This species breeds in Southern Europe, Northern Africa, and Western and Central Asia, especially in Tibet and Yarkand, migrating in winter to India, Assam,

Manipur, and Burma. It is not found on the Malabar Coast, nor in Tenasserim and the Malay countries, though it occurs in China and Japan.

It associates in pairs, though these may combine into flocks, feeding partly on grass, &c., like Geese, and partly on aquatic animals, such as shellfish, and even occasionally on carrion. Rivers are the favourite haunt of these birds, which are very wary, and often troublesome by alarming other birds. Many legends are attached to this showy species, the best known representing them as being inhabited by the spirits of unfortunate lovers, and their loud dissyllabic call certainly does resemble, as Mr. Stuart Baker has pointed out, the Hindustani equivalents for the dialogue *May I come, Chakwa? No, Chakwi, &c.*, which they are supposed to carry on all night. They are not esteemed as food, but can be eaten if skinned previously. In Tibet they breed, generally in May and June, at elevations of 12,000 to 16,000 feet, the nest being in a hole of a bank or cliff. The eggs are white, and the young when hatched appear to be carried to the water by the parents.

The Common Sheldrake.

Tadorna cornuta, BLANFORD, Faun. Brit. Ind., Birds, Vol. IV, p. 427.

VERNACULAR NAMES :—*Shah-Chakwa*, *Safaid Surkhab*, *Raravia*, H.; *Niraji*, Sind; *Chandi Hans*, Calcutta dealers.

This Sheldrake is a smaller bird than the Brahminy, and has a somewhat peculiarly shaped bill, with the profile very concave or "dished" and the nail very small and bent sharply back beneath at an angle; the bill grows much broader towards the tip, where it is furnished with lobes or lips. The male assumes a fleshy knob at the root of the bill in the breeding-season.

The colouration is very striking, being almost the gayest found in any Duck. It is mostly white, but the head is black-green, the wings white, black, green and chestnut, as in the Brahminy; a broad belt of chestnut goes right round the body at the shoulders and lower breast, and the scapulars, tip of tail, and a broad band down the centre of belly below the breast band are black. The stern is chestnut like the breast, but paler.

The bill is scarlet, and the legs flesh-pink. The *female* is like the male, but duller.

The *young* differ from both in having no green on the head, which is brownish black marked with white on the face, and there is no chestnut or black below; moreover the markings above are dull, and the bill and feet pale livid fleshy. But they are recognizably like their parents. The eyes are always dark.

The *male* is about two feet long, with a wing of thirteen inches, and bill and shank about two and-a-quarter. Females are smaller.

The Sheldrake breeds in the north temperate parts of Europe and Asia, migrating south in winter. At this season it is found in Northern India from the Indus Valley to Assam, and occurs also in Upper Burma. It is usually rare, but fairly common in places in Sind. It is essentially a sea-coast bird as a rule; hence probably its rarity in India, though it is more common than is supposed; I used to see one or more in the Calcutta bazaar every year. As it is very bad eating, and quite unmistakable when once seen, it should, I think, be spared by sportsmen, if only on account of its remarkable beauty of form, colour, and movement. It does not bear captivity well in India, though thriving in Europe. The male has a large, double, very thin, bony bulb in the windpipe, and his note is a whistle, while the female barks and quacks. It nests in burrows, either made by itself or appropriated from rabbits, and lays about a dozen yellowish-white eggs.

The so-called EGYPTIAN GOOSE (*Chenalopex aegyptiacus*) is included by M.M. David and Oustalet in their birds of China on the strength of the occurrence of one specimen, but this was probably an escaped bird, as the species is purely African, and often kept and freely bred in captivity, at any rate in Europe, where stray birds are often shot. It is really a large Sheldrake, not a true Goose, though about equal to the Bar-headed Goose in size. Its general colour is a pale brown or creamy-dun, with fine pencillings, with wings coloured as in a Sheldrake, a brown collar round the neck, brown patch round the eye and on the breast, and bright pink bill and legs.

The Comb-Duck.

Sarcidiornis melanonotus, BLANFORD, Faun. Brit. Ind., Birds, Vol. IV, p. 423.

VERNACULAR NAMES.—*Nukta*, H. ; *Nakwa*, Chutia Nagpur ; *Naki hansa*, Uriya ; *Jutu chilluwa*, Tel. ; *Dod sarle haki*, Can. ; *Neer koli*, Coimbatore ; *Tau-bai*, Burma ; *Bowkbang*, Karen.

This although undoubtedly the nearest ally of the dainty little Cotton-teal, is a big, coarse-looking Duck, resembling a Goose in build, and (in the case of the male) in size. The head and feet are large, and the neck, wings, and shanks long. The wings are rounded, the tail almost square, and the bill rather short and high at the root, with the nostrils far forward for a Duck, and the nail large and powerful. The sexes are much alike except in size, but the young bird has a plumage of its own. The male has an upright fleshy comb at the root of the bill, most developed in the breeding season. The *male's* plumage is brilliantly glossed with metallic green, purple and bronze above ; the head and neck are white, speckled with metallic black, the flanks are clear pale grey, and the rest of the underparts white, with frequently a dash of rich yellow on the under tail-coverts at each side. This disappears in skins, and is not always present in the live birds.

The *female* is much like the male in plumage, but duller.

The *young* are brown where the old birds display metallic hues, and have the head and neck marked with brown much after the fashion of the female Cotton-teal, not spotted with black or white.

The eyes, bill, and feet, are all dark, as is the comb when present.

The male is very much larger than the female, measuring about two feet and-a-half, with a wing of fifteen inches, shank two and three-quarters, and bill about the same ; it is much the largest of Indian Ducks proper. The female is not much over two feet long, with a wing about a foot, shank and bill about two inches.

The Comb-duck has a wide range in warm countries and is resident ; it is found in India, Ceylon, and Burma, and also in Africa south of the Sahara and in Madagascar. It is common where there is plenty of wood and water, and rare or wanting in desert tracts. Nor is it common, if it occurs, in the districts south of Mysore, Bombay, the Deccan, Sind, the Western Punjab, and Tenasserim.

This Duck is usually found in small flocks in the cold weather, and at other times in pairs. It is a tree-duck, perching and breeding in trees ; the nest being made in a hole or a fork, of sticks, leaves, feathers, &c. ; the eggs, laid in July, August, or September, are seven to twelve in number, ivory-white and very glossy. In its attitudes on land and water this Duck resembles a Goose, but does not carry the neck so stiffly ; and it flies faster and is a better diver. It is often called the Black-backed Goose, but is not a Goose either in structure, plumage, or habits, keeping much more to the water, and being a very silent bird. It is fairly good eating. The bill is powerful enough to draw blood when the bird is handled, and the slight wound so produced is apt to fester according to my experience. The male has a small bony bulb in the windpipe.

The Cotton-teal.

Nettopus coromandelianus, BLANFORD, Faun. Brit. Ind., Birds, Vol. VI, p. 433.

VERNACULAR NAMES :—*Girria*, *Girri*, *Girja*, *Gurgurra*, Hind. ; *Ghangariel*, *Gangani*, Beng. ; *Bullia-hans*, Dacca, Faridpur, Sylhet ; *Dandana*, Uriya ; *Lerriget-perriget*, *Meromderebet*, Kol ; *Ade*, *Adla*, Ratnagiri ; *Kalagat*, Burmese.

The Cotton-teal, in addition to its very small size, is noticeable for its rather " dumpy " build, short wings, long rounded tail, short legs set far back, and large feet, with strong sharp claws. The bill is almost exactly like that of a Goose in miniature, but has the nostrils near the root ; it tapers to the tip, and has a large nail forming the tip, but at the edges it has the ordinary ridging found in Ducks, not the teeth of a Goose's bill.

The plumage, like the general build, is not at all like that of a Goose, and it differs much in the two sexes, though there is some general correspondence. The *male* is largely white, with the crown metallic dark-brown, a broad black collar below the neck, the upper plumage metallic green and purple ; there is a white patch on the primary quills ; the flanks are pencilled with black, and the under tail-coverts black. The bill is black, the eye red, and the feet black, yellow down the sides of the shanks and toes.

The *female* is brown where the male shows his metallic hues : there is a brown line from the bill through the eye ; the head and neck are speckled with brown and the breast pencilled with that colour ; the flanks are brownish, and the under tail-coverts white, and there is no white patch on the pinion quills. The bill is yellowish brown, the eye dark, and the feet greenish yellow with black webs.

The *young birds* are like the female, and so is the male when in *undress*, except that he retains some green on the wings and the white patch on the quills. This bird is only about a foot in total length, with a wing of about half that, and an inch long bill and shank. It has been called the Goose-teal, Goslet, and Pigmy Goose, but wrongly, as there is nothing goose-like about it except the bill.

The Cotton-teal inhabits the greater part of India, and extends through Burma and the Malay countries to China in one direction and Celebes in another. A large variety of it inhabits Eastern Australia, where also a distinct species is found. It is a resident bird, never leaving the country altogether ; rare in Malabar, the Bombay Presidency, and Kattywar, and absent from desert Rajputana, Sind, and the Western Punjab. It is very abundant in Lower Bengal, but does not now by any means outnumber all the other Ducks in the Calcutta bazaar, as it did in Mr. Hume's time. It prefers well-wooded country with plenty of small ponds and marshes. It is a very fast swimmer and excellent diver, though usually a surface feeder, pecking about more like a Coot or Water-hen than a Duck ; it will dive for food readily enough on occasion, but not very neatly. It is the most active flyer of all our waterfowl, being both swift and nimble; but it is a very poor walker, being although quite able to walk normally, curiously weak in the legs and unwilling to go far at a time; it perches freely. It builds in holes in trees and buildings, laying in July and August a dozen eggs or oftener less, ivory-white and very smooth. The young seem from native evidence quoted by Mr. E. C. Stuart Baker to be carried down in the feet of the old bird ; they are most beautiful and nimble little creatures, clad in dark-brown down with white markings. Cotton-teal moult in autumn, losing all the quills, and it is then that the male goes into *undress*, remaining in this stage during winter. He has no bulb in the windpipe. His note ludicrously resembles the words "Fix bayonets," and is uttered in flight. The flesh is very poor eating in my opinion, not positively objectionable, but flavourless.

The Mandarin Duck.

Aex galericulata, SALVADORI, Brit. Mus. Cat., Birds, Vol. XXVII, p. 76.

VERNACULAR NAMES :—*Oshidori*, Japanese.

The Mandarin Duck, quite apart from the wonderful decorations of the full-plumaged male, is at once distinguishable from all other Indian and Asiatic Ducks by the peculiar form of its wings, which are shaped more like a Pigeon's than a Duck's, the primary quills plainly showing for some distance beyond the short secondaries. In general form it much resembles the Cotton-teal, having a short goose-like bill and rather long rounded tail ; but it also has a full crest, and stands higher on the legs than the Cotton-teal, while the feet are proportionately small ; the eyes are larger than in any other Duck.

The *male* in full plumage is a most extravagantly decorated bird, his general "get up" being suggestive of a Bird-of-Paradise rather than a Duck. His crest, very long and full, is copper-red in front, metallic green behind, and white at the sides, the white also occupying the upper part of the face, but shading into buff as it nears the ruff of bright chestnut hackles which adorns the neck. The breast is purplish-maroon, and the abdomen white. But the wings are the most remarkable part of the bird ; the innermost quill is expanded on its inner side into a chestnut fan three inches broad, while the outer web is of ordinary size and bright steel-blue ;

the pinion-quills are silvery-grey on the outer and steely-blue on the inner webs. There are other elegancies in this little harlequin's plumage, but it would take too much space to describe them here, and the presence of the orange ruff and wing-fans, or of either separately, is quite enough for identification. The bill is rose-red, the eyes dark, and the feet dull orange with black webs.

The *female* is a sober-looking but dainty little bird, but always recognizable by the conspicuous silvery-grey and steely-blue primary quills, which are like those of the male. Her general colour above is plain brown, without any markings, shading to grey on the head and crest. There is a narrow white line round the eye, prolonged back into a streak. Her sides are mottled with creamy-buff, and the abdomen white as in the male. She has a horn-coloured bill and olive feet. The *male in undress* is almost exactly like the female, more so than in any other Duck, which is curious, seeing his extravagance in attire when in full plumage. The white round the eye, however, is less pronounced, and the head greyer. The only easy distinction, however, is the colour of the feet—in a fresh specimen—for they always remain orange in the male; though his bill sometimes turns dull like the female's and sometimes retains the beautiful rose tint of the full dress. *Young males* are like the old male in *undress*, and young females like their mother. The male is about seventeen inches long, with the bill and shank each about one-and-a-quarter, and wing nine and-a-half. This extremely beautiful Duck, though well known as a captive in India—as, probably in all countries where there are Zoological Gardens and fanciers—is a very rare straggler there in the wild state, its proper home being Eastern Siberia, China and Japan. It also visits Amoorland in the summer. It is a very active Duck, a surface-feeder, and very nimble on land, in spite of its affinity to the Cotton-teal. It perches freely, and lays its eggs, which are creamy-white, in holes in trees. Indeed it seems very much of a land and tree-duck, as it is sometimes found in oakwoods, feeding on fallen acorns, and flying up into the trees when disturbed. The male's note is a sort of snorting whistle, the female's a sneezing quack, not loud in either case. The male is much attached to his mate, caresses her like a Pigeon, and constantly shows off his fine plumage before her ; when on the wing, however, all his finery is inconspicuous, and only the broad white eye-brows are noticeable. The only specimen which has occurred wild in India is a female shot out of a flock of six in Assam in March 1902.

The Wigeon.

Mareca penelope,* BLANFORD, Faun. Brit. Ind., Birds, Vol. IV, p. 445.

VERNACULAR NAMES :—*Peasan*, *Patari*, *Pharia Chota-Lalsir*, H.; *Cheyun*, Nepal ; *Parow*, Sind.

The Wigeon is easily distinguished from all other Indian Ducks by its characteristic form. The bill is very short and tapers slightly ; the shanks are also short, and the feet of moderate size. The wings are long and pointed, and the tail is pointed also. The sexes differ absolutely in plumage, and the male in *undress* differs from the female more than is usual with drakes in this stage. The male has a large bony drum in the windpipe.

The *male's* full plumage is of a general pencilled-grey colour, produced by fine black lines on white ; the head

* I have given the specific name of the Wigeon as it is now always written by naturalists ; but it really ought to be *Penelops*, as Gesner and Linnæus had it ; for this is the ancient Greek name of some kind of Duck, probably one with pencilled plumage, since *pene* means a web of cloth in process of weaving and reminds one of our term Canvas-back for the big American Pochard. It could hardly have been the Wigeon, since this was probably the Duck known as *baskas* "the grazer."

is chestnut, with a cream patch from beak to crown; the breast brownish pink; the tail-coverts are black; the "shoulder" of the wing white, as is the belly; the wing-bar on the secondaries metallic green.

The *male in undress* is of a general reddish brown hue, mottled with darker, with blue-grey "shoulders" to the wings, and a white belly.

The *female* is mottled with dark and light brown with a white belly, and has usually no bar on the wing. The young resemble her, but the young male shows some green on the wing.

The bill is French-grey with a black tip, and the feet grey; the eyes dark.

The male measures about nineteen inches, with a bill of an inch and three-quarters and shank a little less. The wing is ten inches long. Females are little smaller.

The Wigeon inhabits Europe, North Africa, and Asia, breeding to the north and migrating southward in winter. It occurs sometimes on the North American coast, but the common Wigeon of North America is a distinct, though closely allied, species, *Mareca americana*.* To India and Burma the Wigeon is a fairly common visitor; it has not been recorded from Ceylon, nor in the Peninsula south of Mysore. It is somewhat local and irregular in its appearance where it occurs; thus Mr. Oates failed to find it in Pegu, though McMaster found it common there, as Hume did in Manipur, and Vidal "in some years" in Ratnagiri. The name Wigeon is often misapplied; for instance, the Ducks so-called in South Africa and Australia are not Wigeon at all.

---

* In this the male has the head buff thickly speckled with black, with a green streak behind the eye, but with the same cream-coloured forehead as our bird; and the dull pink of the breast extends along the flanks. In other respects the plumage is like that of our Wigeon, and females are almost indistinguishable; this species has occurred in Europe, and might possibly do as on the Chinese coast.

The Wigeon is not closely allied to the Ducks with which I have placed it ; its real affinities being with the true Teal, to be treated of later. It differs from these and most other Indian *Anatinæ* in having the habit of grazing like a Goose, for which the short bill is well adapted. In gait and flight, however, this species resembles the ordinary surface-feeding Ducks, and like them is more or less omnivorous at times. It can dive well on occasion. Wigeons are found in flocks, parties, or alone, and frequent salt water as much as fresh ; they are not, in India, among the very best Ducks for the table. The male's note is very characteristic, a loud musical whistle—" whe-ew " ; the female utters a low purring growl. She nests on the ground, and the eggs are creamy-white ; the ducklings begin to graze early, while still tiny downy things.

CHAPTER VII.

True Ducks (*concluded*).

THE other thirteen species of *Anatinæ* with which we have to deal comprise the ordinary surface-feeding Ducks, which do not, as a rule, either dive for food or perch, nor are they found much on land. In all of them the bill is noticeably longer, sometimes considerably, than the shank, which is short, being considerably exceeded in length by the middle toe. The outer toe is, however, not equal to the middle in length, leaving the foot comparatively small. The legs are set rather far back, but not so far as in the diving Ducks, and they walk fairly well, though with a waddling gait. The wings are of good size and pointed, and they fly well. They feed at the surface as a rule, or by reaching down with their tails in the air, seldom diving for food.* They are divided into ten genera, of which three are at once marked of by striking colour, and two by peculiarities of form. The others are separated by characters so trifling that they would be aetter taken all together, their relationship being undoubtedly very close.

Of the peculiarly coloured genera, the sexes of which are recognizably similar,—

The *Wood-duck* is at once distinguished by its large size, dark body, and black and white wings with French-grey bar.

---

* At the same time, I have observed and recorded (Natural Science, 1892, Vol. I, p. 47) that the half-tame Mallards in the London Parks do sometimes dive for food, and also the Mandarin Duck (*Aix galericulata*) and the Chilian Pintail (*Dafila spinicauda*); since this I have even seen the latter bird chasing and catching live fish under water like a Merganser ! This was in St. James' Park, 24th July, 1894.

The *Pink-head* by its dark body, buff quills, and pink or pale drab head.

The *Marbled Teal* by its pale, washed-out-looking plumage, and silver-grey edgings to the pinion-quills.

Of the genera of peculiar form the sexes are very unlike, but the following structural characters distinguish them from all other Indian Ducks of this section.

The *Pintail* has a long sharp tail, half as long as the wing or longer.

The *Shoveller* has a huge mis-shapen bill, very long, and twice as broad at the tip as at the root.

Then come a number of species, referred to several genera, of which the male and female often present hardly any point of colour in common. They may, however, be sorted out partly by size and partly by the colour of the wing-bar.

Of the bigger Ducks, with the wing nine inches or over :—

The *Mallard* and its allies (three species) have a steel-blue or green wing-bar, edged with white.

The *Gadwall* has a white wing-bar and the fringing of the bill showing well below the upper chap.

The *Bronze-cap* has a black or green-black wing-bar and grey feet.

Of the smaller Ducks, or Teal, with the wing under eight and-a-half inches :—

The *Garganey* has the fringing of the bill just showing below the upper chap and the wing-bar dull green or wanting.

The *ordinary Teals* (three species) do not show the fringing of the bill when this is closed, and have the wing-bar black and brilliant green or bronze.

The Wood-duck.

Asarcornis scutulata, BLANFORD, Faun. Brit. Ind., Birds, Vol. IV, p. 424.

VERNACULAR NAME :—*Deo-hans*, Assam.

The Wood-duck is a very big, coarse-looking species which, properly perhaps, occupies a genus to itself, for although of late stated to be allied to the Comb-duck, it presents very many points of difference from that bird. Its beak, besides being longer than the shank, is flatter than the other's, and inclined to widen instead of taper towards the tip, and does not grow a comb. The middle toe is much longer than the shank, instead of only a little, as in the Comb-duck, and the tail is markedly rounded, not nearly square as in that bird. In short, the Wood-duck much more resembles in the matter of form the ordinary Ducks of the Mallard genus (*Anas*). An examination of the drake's windpipe would probably settle the matter.

In colour the *male* is olive-brown above and dull chestnut below, with a white head and neck much spotted with black, and a green-glossed black breast ; the "shoulders" of the wings are white and the wing-bar slate-colour, separated from the white by a black band. The bill is orange or yellow blotched with black, the base becoming, in the male, swollen and red in the breeding-season ; the eyes crimson or brown, and feet orange or yellow.

The *female* is like the male, but with paler bill and feet and considerably smaller. The *male* is over two feet and-a-half long with a fifteen-inch wing, shank nearly two and-a-half and bill nearly three inches. In both sexes the colour varies much according to the freshness of the plumage, newly-moulted birds being very bright and showing much more green gloss than those in old feathering.

This Duck is found as a resident in Assam, the Malay Peninsula and Java, in which last country it is believed to be domesticated. Unlike most of the other Ducks I am including in this section, it is an inveterate percher and haunts water surrounded by jungle. Mr. E. Stuart Baker, our chief authority on this bird, has given some evidence tending to show that this species lays creamy-white eggs in holes of trees, and young birds are said to have been shot on the Dhansiri river in Assam, where this Duck is not rare in the Dibrugarh district; they keep in pairs or small flocks, and have a loud trumpeting call. They are very easily tamed, and Mr. Baker found his specimens would dive and chase live fish under water, a strange habit for a bird of this type, a good walker and quite at home on land.

The Pink-head.

Rhodonessa caryophyllacea, BLANFORD, Faun. Brit. Ind., Birds, Vol. IV, p. 425.

VERNACULAR NAMES :—*Lal sira*, *Golab Lal-sir*, Hind.; *Saknal*, Bengal; *Dumrar*, *Umar*, Nepal Terai and Tirhoot; *Golabi sir*, Calcutta dealers.

Whatever may be the case with the Wood-duck, it is quite certain that the Pink-head stands very much alone among Ducks. It is not very remarkable as to form, being a slight-built Duck, with large but not long wings; a close-feathered, thin and angular-looking head and neck, and an ugly-shaped bill, very flat at the tip, and with the ridges lining it not well developed, but with a large nail.

Its colouring, however, is unique, not only among Ducks but birds in general. The *male's* plumage is generally of a glossy sepia, with buff wing-bar, and the pinion-quills also shaded internally with buff; the head and neck, with the exception of a broad black band down the throat and front of the neck, are of a most crude and brilliant rose-pink, which does not harmonize at all well with the bright red eye, and white beak shading into flesh colour at base and tip.

The *female*, though less striking in appearance, much resembles the male. She is, however, duller throughout, the pink of the head being especially dull and dirty; there is no black on the throat, but a black streak along the crown. This mark the male assumes when not in full colour. The bill of the female is black, with a cream bar between nostrils and root; eye duller than in male. The *young* are much like the female, but paler below, and with the head of a dull neutral tint instead of pink. The bill probably resembles that of the female in all young birds, but the youngest male I have seen already has a light bill in the skin; and even in skins the difference in colour in the bills still shows. The feet are purplish black in all. The male is about two feet long, with a wing about eleven inches, shank nearly two, and bill all but two and-a-half. The female is a little smaller.

The Pink-head is a purely Indian Duck, never leaving our area, nor occurring outside it. In most places it is rare, but fairly common in Upper Bengal in the districts of Purneah, Maldah, Bhagulpur, and in Tirhoot; in the rest of Bengal, Orissa, the Northern Circars, Oudh, and the North-West Provinces it occurs but rarely, and may straggle occasionally to Delhi, Mhow, and Ahmednagar on the west and Madras on the south; while from the east it has been recorded north of Bhamo. It frequents, in small or moderate-sized flocks, weedy ponds and swamps, generally those surrounded by jungle, and nests on the ground in high grass in June and July. The eggs are quite unique, white and nearly spherical in shape; about nine are laid. The male's windpipe has a most curious bulb, partly of bone and partly of membrane, the latter being supported by fine network of bone ; his note is low, musical, and quite unlike that of any other Duck, resembling the syllabes "*wugh-ah!*" The flight is light and easy, and the habits those of a true surface-feeder, though there can be little doubt that the real relationships of this bird are with the Pochards on account of the colour of the wing and the structure of the windpipe. It is poor eating as a rule, and being so very striking and interesting a bird, should, I think, be perpetually protected ; though specimens might be legitimately captured for home fanciers, who have never yet, I believe, succeeded in breeding it.

The Marbled Teal.

Marmaronetta angustirostris, BLANFORD, Faun. Brit. Ind., Birds, Vol. IV, p. 454.

VERNACULAR NAMES :—None known.

This is a small, slightly-built Duck, with a short full crest and a long narrow parallel-sided bill. Its peculiar coarsely-mottled mealy-looking plumage will at once distinguish it from any other Duck ; it shows two colours only, greyish brown and dirty white, with the exception of a wash of silver grey on the outside of the pinion-quills. The darker colour predominates above, and the lighter below, and there is no wing-bar ; the bill is grey and black, the eyes dark, and the feet dark or grey.

The *female* only differs from the *male* in being smaller, duller, and with less crest. The male is about a foot and-a-half long, with a wing of about eight inches, shank just under one and-a-half and bill just over two.

This Duck, which looks like a semi-albino of some other species, inhabits Southern Europe, especially Spain, Northern Africa, and South-Western Asia. In India it is chiefly known as a winter visitor to Sind, but it has occurred in the South-West Punjab, Bahawalpur, Northern Guzerat, Rajputana, the North-West Provinces, and Oudh, and near Calcutta. In Sind it affects rush-covered swamps, where it occurs in large numbers, the birds rising two or three at a time when disturbed, not all at once like most Ducks. It is said both to whistle and to quack: probably the voices of the sexes are different, as is so usually the case. It is probable, but not absolutely certain, that it breeds in Sind. The eggs are yellowish white, about ten in number, and the nest is placed on the ground among rushes in the countries where the bird breeds. Although differing so little from the female in outward appearance, the male of this species yet possesses the bony bulb in the windpipe so often found in drakes.

In the other species belonging to this section, the males in *undress*, females and young have the plumage mottled with light and dark in a very characteristic way, and some look much alike at first; but they are much easier to discriminate than young Pochards. Two of the genera are also, as remarked above, easily known by peculiarities of form, and the others may generally be distinguished by the colour of the wing-bar, which is different in each species, and common to all members thereof as a rule. The reason for the existence of this natural coat-of-arms is an interesting subject for speculation.

A theory has been advanced to the effect that the differing markings on the wings of allied birds are "recognition marks" whereby the individuals of each species are enabled to know their own kind, and hence verify the proverb about birds of a feather flocking together. There may be something in this, as it is obviously important that all the birds in a flock should keep "time" and observe formation in their evolutions, and so the occasional occurrence of alien individuals in flocks of other species cannot be held to be a serious objection to the theory. Nevertheless, the Ducks, which furnish such excellent examples of differing wing-markings, also furnish evidence which is rather unfavourable to this recognition-colour idea. In the first place, several of the Pochards agree in having the same wing-pattern, and the flight of these is certainly not quite the same. And secondly, the wing-bar is not *always* constant in the same species in all its individuals ; the female Wigeon, as we have seen, seldom has one, and it is generally absent in the female Pintail, though I knew at one time in India of no less than three female individuals of this species which acquired it, though without it at first. Also the female Garganey gets an approach to this marking with advancing age ; so that it would seem that these two species are now acquiring the marking, which is not yet fixed. But if it were so important to the birds to know each other, the slower, weaker females would need to show their nationality more than the males, the more so as they are especially the members of the species which are so difficult to distinguish as to render a special recognition-mark necessary. In favour of considering the marking as an ornament is the fact that it is in some cases at any rate displayed in courtship, and this is, no doubt, the chief use of its presence.

The Shoveller.

Spatula clypeata, BLANFORD, Faun. Brit. Ind., Birds, Vol. IV, p. 452.

VERNACULAR NAMES :—*Tidari*, *Punana*, *Tokarwala*, *Ghirah*, H. ; *Pantamukhi*, Beng. ; *Dhobaha Sankhar* (male), *Khikeria Sankhar* (female), Nepal ; *Alipat*, Sind.

The Shoveller's one point—it can hardly be said of beauty, but of generic distinction from other Ducks—is its very large and curiously formed bill. This is twice as long as the shank, and twice as broad near the tip

(Page 104) H. Grönvold, del.

Common Teal.

Page 101) H. Grönvold, del.

Garganey.

as at the root, with the sides of the upper chap much turned down near the end, and furnished with a very deep and conspicuous fringe, forming a very perfect sifting apparatus. For the rest, it is a light-built Duck, with long pointed wings and rather small feet.

The *male's* head and neck are bright metallic green, the lower neck and breast white, belly and flanks bay followed by a white patch, rump and stern black-green, long pointed scapulars blue, black and white; the wings very bright, with blue shoulders and bright green bar bordered in front with white. The bill is black, eye yellow and feet orange.

The *female* is mottled dark and light brown, with a general tawny hue; the wing has a grey or grey brown shoulder and the wing-bar is duller green than in the male. Her bill is brown above, orange below, and her eyes brown. The *young* are like her, and the *male in undress* is similar, except for being darker and redder in hue, and retaining his brilliant wing-colouring.

The male is about twenty inches long, with a wing rather over nine, bill about three, and shank about one and-half. The female is smaller.

The Shoveller inhabits the greater part of the northern hemisphere, breeding in the temperate portion, and migrating south in winter, when it visits India, Ceylon and Northern Burma among other places. It becomes rarer to the southward than in Northern India, but is reported by a writer in the Rangoon Gazette, Nov. 26, 1908, as not rare in Pegu or Tenasserim, and Mr. Oates has obtained a specimen from the Shan States. It does not ordinarily breed in India, but Layard found young birds in Ceylon, so it must sometimes do so. The nest is on the ground, and the eggs greenish buff. In India it haunts fresh water and is found singly or in small numbers, keeping to the shallows, for it is of all the Ducks most perfectly adapted for surface feeding. Captive birds have been noticed to assiduously sift the water above feeding Pochards; this I never saw done by a bird I long possessed, but I have observed the same habit in tame Teal (*Nettium crecca*) in England. The Shoveller is fond of dirty little village ponds, where it is very tame, and is said to be a very foul feeder; its flesh is considered poor in India, but I must say the only one I ever ate was good enough, and in America, Audubon said that no good judge would pass a Shoveller to shoot a Canvas-back. The male Shoveller has a small bony bulb in the windpipe; his note is a harsh short croak. It is interesting to note that when first hatched the duckling of this species has an ordinary-looking bill, and that the young drakes show the enlargement most as growth proceeds.

The Pintail.

Dafila acuta, BLANFORD, Faun. Brit. Ind., Birds, Vol. IV, p. 447.

VERNACULAR NAMES :—*Sanh*, *Sink-par*, H. (N.-W. P.); *Kokarali*, *Drighush*, Sind; *Dig-hans*, *Sho-lon-cho*, Beng.; *Digunch*, Nepal; *Nanda*, *Nanja*, Uriya; *Laitunga*, Manipur; *Tau-bay*, Burm.

The Pintail, despite its strikingly aristocratic appearance, has really but the faintest claim to generic rank. Its only peculiarity consists in its slender build, with long neck, long parallel-sided bill, and long pointed tail, of which the centre feathers in drakes reach a great length. The wings are also long, but the legs remain rather short.

The *male's* plumage is of a general pencilled-grey colour on the upper surface and flanks, produced by fine black lines on white; the head is dull dark brown with a lilac gloss on each side behind the eyes; the back of the neck black, with a white band on each side running down to join the white of the fore-neck, breast and belly; the stern and long tail-feathers are black, and just in front of the tail, on the flank, is a yellow-buff patch. The wing-bar is bronze-green, with a cinnamon bar in front and a white one behind. The scapulars are long, and black with pale edges.

The *female* is mottled with dark brown and buff or white, the markings being particularly clear and distinct; she usually shows no coloured wing-bar, but two whitish ones where it should be. In both sexes the bill is black along the middle and grey at the sides, the eyes dark, and the feet grey. *Young birds* have darker and more uniformly-coloured bills.

The *male in undress* bears a general resemblance to the female, but the details of the marking are different, the light bars being nearly transverse, instead of following the outline of the feather; and he shows the wing-bar as in full plumage. The young male appears to resemble him in this stage.

The *male* is about two feet long, but may be more or less according to the development of his long tail-feathers, which may measure over nine inches; he has an eleven-inch wing, bill about two and-a-half inches, and shank over one and-a-half. The *female* is smaller and has a much shorter and less pointed tail, though this is still long for a Duck, and the transversely-barred feathers thereof are characteristic of her only.

Pintails have an exceedingly wide range, being found nearly all over the Northern Hemisphere; in the United States they are known as "Sprigs." They breed mostly near the Arctic circle, nesting on the ground and laying greenish-grey eggs, and are only winter visitants to our area, occurring throughout India, Burma, and Ceylon. They are generally in flocks which are sometimes very large, and frequently composed of males only. They are remarkably rapid flyers, but do not rise so easily as might be expected from their light build. The male has a bony bulb in the windpipe, and his voice is a faint soft note, while the female utters a harsh unpleasant quack; but they are silent birds as a rule, the females especially. They are always most excellent eating, and as they stand the hot weather well, might easily be kept through the summer for table purposes in any suitable tank or building. This species is particularly liable to show the rusty wash on the lower parts found in many Ducks; it is undoubtedly a stain, as a drake Pintail I had unpinioned showed it suddenly one day after a night's absence from the tank where he was living.

I once saw a semi-albino Pintail drake in the Calcutta bazaar, of a pallid whitish hue with flesh-coloured bill and feet; and Mr. M. Mackenzie, of Chuprah, wrote me once that he had got a snow-white female of this bird.

The Mallard, Spot-bill, and Yellow-nib are large Ducks of a somewhat heavy build, with big broad bills; they are about the same size, but are easily distinguished by the wing-marking; the wing-bar is steel-blue in the Mallard and Yellow-nib, in the Spotted-bill metallic green with a long white splash above and behind it.

The Mallard.

Anas boscas, BLANFORD, Faun. Brit. Ind., Birds, Vol. IV, p. 435.

VERNACULAR NAMES:—*Nil-sir*, *Niroji*, H.; *Lilg* (male), *Lilgahi* (female), Nepal.

The Mallard differs from all our Ducks in that the male's four middle tail-feathers are curled up; he is very different from the female in general plumage also. In general colour the *male* is grey, the effect being produced by a fine pencilling of dark brown on white, more or less marked: the head is bright metallic green, this colour

(Page 90) H. Grönvold, del.

Pintail.

(Page 92) H. Grönvold, del.

Mallard.

being separated by a white ring round the middle of the neck from the deep bay of the lower neck and breast; the rump, stern, and curly tail-feathers are black, and the wing-bar steel-blue edged with white fore and aft. The bill is yellowish olive-green and the feet orange; eyes dark.

The *female* is mottled with light and dark brown, with the wings and feet like the male; her bill is commonly black with an orange tip and edges, but varies. The *male in undress* is like her, but black on crown and rump; young males resemble him in this stage.

The *male* is about two feet long, with a wing about eleven inches; bill about two and-a-half, and shank about one and-a-half; the female is smaller and considerably lighter.

The Mallard, like many others of our Ducks, has a very wide range, being a resident throughout the temperate regions of the Northern Hemisphere; some birds migrate south in winter. With us it breeds in the Himalayas and Kashmir, and in winter is common in the Western Punjab and Sind, not rare in the North-West Provinces, Oudh and Behar, and occasionally occurs in Guzerat, the Central India Agency, the Deccan, Bengal, Assam, and Northern Burma; in Southern India, Ceylon, Pegu, and Tenasserim it is unknown. Although by no means widely or universally distributed over India, this is the most familiar of all Ducks, being the common wild species of Europe, and the ancestor of our various tame breeds, except the Muscovy, which comes from a very distinct South American bird (*Cairina moschata*), a tree-haunting species more nearly allied to our Comb-duck. The domestication of the Duck is not so very ancient, since Columella, a Roman agricultural writer of about the beginning of the Christian era, recommends that Ducks should be kept in netted enclosures to prevent their flying away, and that the stock should be increased by taking the eggs of the wild birds and putting them under hens—showing that Ducks were about as much domesticated then as Pheasants are now ; a fact which makes their general loss of the power of flying, while this has been retained by the Goose, particularly interesting. The Mallard is, indeed, one of the easiest of all birds to tame and breed ; it also crosses very freely with other Ducks, and stamps its impress on the hybrid in a very noticeable way, as far as coloration is concerned. Those who require a large Duck for the table out here should not try to introduce the heavy European breeds, which are unsuited to the country, but cross the country Ducks with the Muscovy, by which means a large Duck is produced, weighing over six pounds, and of excellent flavour. It is of course barren, but there is no difficulty in making the cross as often as required. The wild Mallard is one of the best of all Ducks for the table, though remarkably omnivorous in its habits ; it is usually found in small or large flocks. The *male* has a bony drum in the windpipe, and any one who has noticed poultry must have observed the difference in the voice of the sexes, the drake's hoarse faint quack sounding as if he had a very bad cold. The Mallard breeds in Kashmir in May and the first half of June, laying six to a dozen greenish white eggs in a nest of grass, &c., on the ground. In England it not unfrequently builds in trees, the young ones being allowed to fall and take their chance.

The Spotted-bill.

Anas pœcilorhyncha, BLANFORD, Faun. Brit. Ind., Birds, Vol. IV, p. 436.

VERNACULAR NAMES :—*Garm-pai*, *Garmpar*, *Bata*, *Gugral*, H. ; *Hunjur*, Sind ; *Naddun*, Nepal Terai ; *Kara*, Manipur ; *Tau-bay*, Burmese.

In the Spotted-bill the male and female are alike, and

the wings are proportionately shorter than in the Mallard; the Spotted-bill, however, stands higher on its legs. The general plumage is mottled light and dark, much as in the females of other Ducks of this section, with a general greyish cast. The fore-part of the body is mostly light, the hinder dark, the rump and stern being quite black. The wing-bar is metallic green, edged white fore and aft, and the outer webs of the inner quills are white, making a long white splash on the wing; this is often stained with brown in the female. The bill is very characteristic, orange or scarlet at the root, black for most of its length, and broadly tipped with brilliant yellow varying to orange; in fact, Mr. F. Gleadow told me that in Sind he has found the tip and root of the bill about the same colour; here in Bengal they are very different. The eyes are dark, and feet bright red, varying to orange, the old males having them brightest. The female is not much smaller than the male in this species.

Young birds are less spotted below and, when first fledged, usually have the black of the bill not reaching the sides, and the red patches only indicated by an orange shading at the base, the sides of the bill being yellow. In some, however, the black spreads right across the bill, and the two basal red patches are defined, much earlier than in others.

The Spotted-bill is always confined to the Indian Empire, and is found throughout India south of the Himalayas, Assam, Manipur, the Upper Irrawaddy Valley above Mandalay, and the Shan States, but is rare in Lower Burma. In Ceylon it is found, but is not common. It frequents fresh water, and is found, according to season, in pairs or small parties, as a rule. The breeding-season for this species varies according to locality, being in Northern India generally from July to September.

The eggs are greyish-white, and six to twelve in number, and the nest, made of grass and rushes, is placed on the ground in cover or on a low branch of a tree. The Spotted-bill flies as quickly as the Mallard, and swims and dives better, being very hard to catch if wounded; its note, in both sexes, is much like that of this its ally. It has been introduced into European collections of waterfowl, and breeds well, sometimes hybridizing with the Mallard; and this hybrid is at least partly fertile. But the intermixture of these two very beautiful and distinct species is strongly to be deprecated, except for the purpose of a scientific experiment.

It would appear that the female Spotted-bill prefers the Mallard to her own drakes, for on two occasions, on Mr. W. Rutledge's premises, a Spotted-bill Duck has mated with a Mallard-coloured tame drake, in spite of the presence of males of her own species; in one case eggs were laid, and in the other, the birds were several times seen to pair.

The Yellow-nib.

Anas zonorhyncha, SALVADORI, British Museum Catalogue of Birds, Vol. XXVII, p. 211.

This Duck is very like the Spotted-bill, but has a blue wing-bar like the Mallard, with no white in front of it, and very little white on the tertiaries; there is no red on the bill, and the yellow tip of this is smaller than in the Spotted-bill; and the whole belly is dark, while in that species it is light and spotted down to the thighs. The *female* is paler than the *male*, and the *young* are lighter still, and resemble the Spotted-bill in having a white border in front of the wing-bar and a considerable amount of white on the tertiaries.

In the *Asian* for January 10th, 1899, page 376, "Earth-worm," writing from Kengtung, South Shan States, enumerated 24 *A. zonorhyncha* as shot there in the previous year, and showed that it bred there. Its usual breeding place is North-East Asia, including

Japan, and the eggs are ivory white. Since then Mr. H. N. Thompson (Journal, As. Soc., Bengal, Vol. LXIX, pt. II, pp. 141, 142) has recorded it as common in these States, and as meeting at the Fort Stedman lake with the Spotted-bill, hybrid birds often occurring in this locality. A specimen of the Spotted-bill from Tamilone, Upper Burma, and another from Yunnan, collected by the late Dr. J. Anderson and in the Indian Museum in my time, showed no red on the bill, though adult, and might have had some *zonorhyncha* blood. At the same time observers will need to be careful in imputing a hybrid origin to intermediate specimens, since, as above noted, the young Yellow-nibs are much more like the Spotted-bill than their parents, though the blue wing-bar ought to distinguish them. The Yellow-nib also has a proportionately longer wing; it inhabits China, Japan and the Kurile Islands, Mongolia and Eastern Siberia, and has full claim to rank as one of our Indian Ducks, as in addition to the above records, several collectors have met with it from 1901 onwards in the Dibrugarh district.

The Australian Wild Duck.

Anas superciliosa, SALVADORI, Brit. Mus. Cat., Birds, Vol. XXVII, p. 206.

This Duck which is the "Black Duck" of Australia and "Grey Duck" of New Zealand sportsmen closely resembles the Mallard and Spotted-bill in size, form, note, and general habits. Its colour, however, is noticeably different, being of a very dark chocolate brown with narrow paler edgings to the feathers; the sides of the head are buff, with a very distinct black eye-streak, and the wing-bar is metallic green with black edgings fore and aft. The bill is slate-colour and the feet dull orange. There is no sex difference, both drake and duck having the same sombre plumage, which reminds one of the dark brown often seen in tame Ducks. Although occurring as near the Indian Empire as Java, and ranging through the East Indies, this is essentially a Pacific-region species, being the common wild Duck not only of Australia and New Zealand, but of New Guinea and even Polynesia, where very few Ducks are found. It lays about a dozen eggs of a creamy or greenish-white, but, though so very similar to the Mallard and Spotted-bill in most respects—indeed, it will in captivity interbreed with them with the greatest readiness—it is much more of a tree-builder, the nest being placed indifferently either on the ground or in a hole or stump of a tree or in the deserted nest of some other bird.

The Gadwall.

Chaulelasmus streperus, BLANFORD, Faun. Brit. Ind., Birds, Vol. IV, p. 440.

VERNACULAR NAMES :—*Mila*, *Bhuar*, *Beykhur*, H. ; *Peing-hans*, Beng. ; *Mail*, Nepal ; *Burd*, Sind.

The Gadwall, though one of the larger Ducks, is a delicately formed bird, with long wings, small feet, and a narrow bill, of which the fringing shows well below the upper chap.

The *male* has the head and neck closely speckled brown, the breast mottled black and white ; the general plumage brownish-grey, the effect produced by a pencilling of black and buff ; the belly is white, the rump and stern are black, and the wing-bar is white behind with a black patch before ; there is an ill-defined patch of deep chestnut on the flat of the wing. The bill is black and the feet orange, more or less dull, with black webs ; the eyes dark.

The *female* is mottled dark and light brown, with a white belly, the wing-bar is like that of the male, but there is only a little chestnut on the wing. The feet and legs are like the male's, but the bill is orange at the sides to a greater or less extent as a rule, though not invariably.

Young birds and *males in undress* resemble the female, but the former are more spotted below, and the wing-

(Page 98) H. Grönvold, del.

Gadwall.

(Page 94) H. Grönvold, del.

Spotted-bill.

coloration is not distinct ; their narrow, well-fringed bill and orange-tinged feet will, however, distinguish them from any other species. The *male in undress* retains the wing-colours. The male is about twenty inches long with a wing about ten, bill about two, and shank about one and-a-half. Females are smaller.

The Gadwall, like several of the Ducks of this section, ranges through the greater part of the Northern Hemisphere, breeding in the temperate zone. In winter it is common in Northern India, to Assam, Manipur, and Upper Burma, but it is not known to reach Pegu, Tenasserim, the Peninsula south of Mysore, or Ceylon. It is a common bird in the Northern India, frequenting fresh water in general in large or small flocks. It is more active and graceful in its movements than the Mallard or Spotted-bill, and more noisy, though the call is weaker. Gadwalls are usually good eating, but may at times be ill-flavoured, as recorded by "Chain-Snaffle" in *The Asian*, December 20th, 1898, page 301. The male has a bony bulb in the windpipe, but I am not aware how his voice differs from that of the female, as I presume it does. There was in the Indian Museum a very curious hybrid between this species and the Mallard, which was obtained in the Calcutta bazaar. In plumage it much resembles a male Teal (*Nettium crecca*), but its large size, yellow feet, and the chestnut and white on the wing show its relationship to be rather with this species.

The Bronze-Cap.

Eunetta falcata, BLANFORD, Faun. Brit. Ind., Birds, Vol. IV, page 438.

VERNACULAR NAMES :—*Kala Sinkhur*, Oudh.

This bird, rather unjustly set down as a Teal, for it is of very fair size, certainly does not deserve generic distinction from the Gadwall, which it most resembles in size and build, though not showing the fringing of the bill externally.

The male only shows remarkable peculiarities. These are a bushy, silky, mane-like crest, long sabre-shaped tertiaries, and tail-coverts so ample as to cover the tail completely. The female is quite an ordinary-looking Duck.

The *male's* head is bronze and green ; the throat and fore neck white with a dark green collar below the middle ; the body plumage resembles that of the Gadwall, with a coarsely mottled breast and finely pencilled body, but the colours are pure black and white, making a clear delicate grey in combination. The wings are plain grey with a black-green bar ; the rump black, and the stern black in the middle and yellow-buff at the sides. The long hanging plumes in the wings are black with pale grey borders, and do not show till the rest of the male plumage is fully developed. The bill is black, the eyes dark, and the feet grey. The *female* is almost exactly like the female Gadwall, but the wing-bar is black, sometimes edged with white, and the feet grey, so that she can easily be distinguished from that bird. The bill is also entirely black, while the Gadwall's is orange below at all events. The *young* and the *male in undress* resemble the female, but the latter shows some green gloss on the head.

The Bronze-cap is common in Eastern Asia, breeding in Siberia, where it nests on the ground, and lays up to ten cream-coloured eggs, and wintering to the southward in China, Japan, &c. To the westward it is rare, though it even extends to Europe at times ; but it occasionally visits India and Upper Burma in winter ; it has also twice occurred in Manipur.* No doubt the female often gets passed over as a female Gadwall ; and during my time we had quite a rush of this species, as we had of Bær's

* A specimen procured there was in the Indian Museum, presented by the late proprietor of *The Asian.*

Pochard, for during the cold weather of 1898-99, I got no less than six specimens, four females and two males, from the Calcutta bazaar, whence I had got a male in 1897. During the cold weather of 1899-1900, the species was quite common in the bazaar ; I saw about a dozen, all females with the exception of two, a quite immature and a nearly full-plumaged male. Mr. C. M. Inglis also procured a male in Tirhut, on January 18th, 1900 ; and Mr. M. Mackenzie wrote me that he had got four specimens in Chapra, three males and a female. In the winter of 1900-1901 the bird turned up again in fair numbers, although the season was a very bad one for wildfowl, and I saw only a few Bær's Pochards. In January and February 1902, I noted as many as sixteen, but most of those I saw were females. Any one getting hold of living specimens of this very beautiful and unmistakable Duck should keep them alive for some zoological collection. In India, it usually appears in very small numbers, but probably occurs in flocks when it is common as elsewhere. One of my drakes uttered a cry, when frightened, like an ordinary duckling. There is a small bony bulb in the windpipe of the male, and the female's note is different, being a quack much like that of the female common Wild Duck.

The Garganey or Blue-winged Teal.*

Querquedula circia, BLANFORD, Faun. Brit. Ind., Birds, Vol. IV., p. 449.

VERNACULAR NAMES :—*Chaitwa*, *Khaira*, *Patari*, H. ; *Ghang-roib*, *Giria*, Bengal.

With this species we begin the series of Teals, which are all birds of small size. The present one's only strik-

* This is the usual name given to this species in India by sportsmen, but the *real* Blue-winged Teal (*Querquedula discors*) is a North American bird, which has visited Europe a few times and may turn up in China. In it the male has the shoulders really blue, like the Shoveller's and the head lavender with a white vertical crescent between bill and eye.

ing point is that the fringing of the bill just shows below the upper chap, the blue wing being confined to the male.

The *male's* colouration is very complicated, but he can always be recognized by his pinky-brown head closely speckled with white, with black crown and large white eyebrow : the breast, rump and stern are mottled brown and black ; the wing "shoulders" are lavender grey, and the wing-bar dull light metallic green with a broad white border fore and aft ; the belly is white and the flanks white, coarsely pencilled with black ; the long pointed scapulars are streaked with French grey, black and white. The eyes are brown, and the bill and feet purplish grey. Mr. E. C. Stuart Baker, however, has met with one specimen with orange feet.

The *female* is mottled with dark brown and whitish, and has no wing-bar, or a very faint indication of one. The eyes, bill and feet resemble those of the male.

The *male in undress* is exactly like the female except for the wings. He is later than most other Ducks in acquiring the full dress, not being in perfect plumage till the end of winter. The long scapulars are the last part of the male plumage to develop. *Young males* resemble him. The male is about sixteen inches long, with a wing about seven and-a-half, shank rather over one, and bill about one-and-three-quarters. Females are smaller.

The Garganey appears to be peculiarly liable to albinism. I have observed no less than six of a peculiar pallid variety, showing more or less of the usual markings in a pale washed-out shade. A pair of these are shown in the Bird Gallery of the Indian Museum, the male of which lived for some years in the Calcutta Zoo ; and I exhibited another pair, obtained in the bazaar, to the Asiatic Society. Since then a skin of an almost pure white specimen was submitted to me for identification, the bill and feet of which had evidently been dark in life. But this was an exception, for the feet and bill of these albinistic birds, as far as I have been able to observe, are flesh-coloured, and hence they ought never to be mistaken for the Marbled Teal, which has dark bill and feet, and is besides a much larger bird and very differently marked, the mottlings being very coarse. Our Blue-winged Teal has a wide range in the old world, breeding through a great part of the temperate zone in Europe and Asia, and wintering in North Africa, North China and Southern Asia as far as the Philippines and Celebes. It is one of our commonest winter visitants, occurring throughout India, Ceylon and Burma. It arrives early and leaves late, and is almost always in flocks, often large. It occasionally breeds with us, as young have been obtained in Oudh and at Moulmein. The eggs are creamy-white, six to thirteen in number, and deposited in a grass nest lined with down on the ground. The Garganey is a good bird for the table, if not quite equal to the Common Teal, and like that bird thrives excellently in confinement if suitable accommodation be provided, standing the hot weather well. The male has a peculiar inward guttural croak; he is provided with a bony bulb in the windpipe, larger than that present in the Common Teal, and differently formed.

The Common Teal and its allies, the Clucking and the Andaman Teal, are placed together in one genus (*Nettium*), though they differ considerably *inter se*, especially the last named. They are all small delicately formed Ducks, with the bill not showing the fringing below the edges of the upper chap, and they all have a wing-bar of black and metallic-green or bronze. Independently of the difference of size and proportions they may be easily distinguished by this marking, as follows :—

The *Common Teal* has the wing-bar half black and half green longitudinally, with a broad white or buff-and-white border in front.

The *Clucking Teal* has it bordered narrowly in front with cinnamon, and then half black and half green transversely.

The *Andaman Teal* has the wing-bar velvety-black, with a bronze or bronze-green streak running through it longitudinally, and a big white patch in front.

The Common Teal.

Nettium crecca, BLANFORD, Faun. Brit. Ind., Birds, Vol. IV, p. 443.

VERNACULAR NAMES:—*Chota Murghabi*, *Kerra*, *Lohya Kerra*, *Putari*, *Souchuruka*, H.; *Naroib*, *Tulsia-bigri*, Beng.; *Baigilagairi*, Nepal; *Kardo*, Sind.; *Killowai*, Tamil; *Sorlai-haki*, Can.

This Teal is the smallest of its genus, and with the exception of the Cotton Teal, our smallest Duck. It has for its size a large head and bill, the latter narrow and nearly parallel-sided; otherwise it is a very delicately formed little creature.

The *male* is pencilled-grey in general colour, being marked with fine black lines on a white ground; the head is chestnut, with a broad metallic-green stripe bordered with cream colour running back from the eye. The breast is buff with round black spots; the belly white; the scapulars and stern black and cream, and the wing-bar very brilliant metallic-green above, velvet-black below, with a buff and white anterior border, and a white edging behind. The bill is black, eyes brown, and feet grey.

The *female* is mottled with dark brown and whitish, but has the wing-bar like that of the male, only not quite o bright, and with no buff; by it she can easily be distinguished from the very similar female Blue-winged Teal, as well as by her narrower bill not showing the

(Page 69) H. Grönvold, del.

Brahminy Duck.

(Page 74) H. Grönvold, del.

Cotton-teal.

fringe, and rather smaller size. Eyes, feet and bill as in the male, but the last not so black.

The *male in undress* bears a general resemblance to the female, but, as in the Pintail, differs in details of marking. *Young birds* resemble the female, but are more spotted below. Probably young males are like the male in undress.

The male is about fifteen inches long, with a wing of about seven and-a-half, bill about one-and-three-quarters and shank just over the inch. Females are not much smaller.

This Teal has a wider range than the Blue-winged, not only inhabiting Europe, North Africa, and Asia, in the temperate portions of which it breeds, laying some times more than a dozen ivory-coloured eggs in a nest on the ground, straggles at times to the East Coast of North America, on which continent it is, however, generally replaced by a very similar species, the American green-winged Teal, *Nettium carolinense*. It is a very common winter visitor to India, and probably occurs over the whole of our area, as it ranges as far as the Philippines, although not yet recorded from South Tenasserim. It keeps generally in small flocks, or even may be found in pairs or singly, on small pieces of water as well as large, unlike the Garganey. It has a smarter flight than that bird, and is better eating, both wild and tame. It stands captivity equally well, and is easily kept. I have noticed individuals of this species kept in the Duck Aviary at the Calcutta Zoological Garden, which had acquired the habit of perching like Tree-ducks on the narrow ridges of gable-topped nesting-boxes—a thing Blue-winged Teal confined with them never seemed to do. This Teal whistles and quacks, the female being responsible for the latter sound and the male for the former; he has, as above implied, a bony bulb to the windpipe.

The Clucking Teal.

Nettium formosum, BLANFORD, Faun. Brit. Ind., Birds, Vol. IV, p. 442.

VERNACULAR NAMES :—None known.

This species is considerably larger than the Common Teal, but has a proportionately much shorter and broader bill ; the male also has long pointed scapulars like the Blue-winged Teal.

The *male's* plumage is somewhat complicated to describe, but he cannot easily be mistaken for any other Duck, by reason of his buff head, with black crown separated by a white line from the metallic green streak passing back from the eye, and black throat sending up a black streak on each side to the lower eyelid. The back and rump are grey-brown, with an area of delicate blue-grey, formed by minute black and white lines, on each side of the shoulders, while pencilling re-appears on the flanks. The long pointed scapulars are chestnut, buff, and black, and the breast pinky-buff, darker at the sides and with black round spots in the middle. The belly is white, and the stern mostly black with chestnut edges and preceded by a white bar. The wing-bar shows first a cinnamon band, then a bronze-green one, then a black, and is finished off with white. The tertials are edged with buff.

The *female* resembles the male in the colour of the wings ; otherwise she is mottled grey-brown, very like the female Common and Blue-winged Teal. But the wing-markings alone will easily distinguish her, to say nothing of the larger size with proportionately short bill, this being no longer than in the Common Teal.

The *male in undress* is like the female, but with a redder breast and plain back. When nearly in full plumage the head-markings are dulled by fine brown edgings to every feather, though still quite distinguishable.

The bill is dark bluish-grey, the eyes brown, and the feet blue-grey or olive; but in the female I got in Calcutta, the beak was olive at the root, spotted with black, and black at the tip, as well as having the feet olive-yellow with grey webs. But this was an exceptional specimen, as she had the plumage of the male in undress, although, on dissection, the eggs in her ovary were plainly perceptible.

The *male* is about sixteen inches long, with a wing about eight, bill about one-and-three-quarters, and shank about one-and-a-half. The female is little smaller.

This very beautiful Teal properly belongs to Eastern Siberia, China, and Japan, breeding in the north of this area; occasionally, however, it straggles to the westward even as far as Europe. In India it is excessively rare, only about four instances of its occurrence having been recorded till the cold weather of 1898-99, when I got the above-mentioned female in the Calcutta bazaar, and Mr. M. Mackenzie of Rajaputtee, Chuprah, a male in the Sarun District, both of which were reported in *The Asian*; on 16th December 1898, Mr. E. L. Barton, of Bombay, shot a male about twenty miles from Ahmedabad in Guzerat; and since then the Indian Museum has received the head of a male, shot at Jaipur, on April 6th, 1899, by Mr. C. Barker. Another was shot in the district of Dibrugarh by Colonel Row.

The Calcutta female, the only one of that sex hitherto recorded from India, was in my time exhibited in the Bird Gallery of the Indian Museum along with the first recorded Indian specimen, a full-plumaged male obtained, also in the Calcutta bazaar, by Blyth in 1844, and then, alas! in very poor condition. This is therefore a bird to be looked out for, as no doubt there are and have been more about; though it must be noticed that the last few years have been unusually remarkable for an invasion of

India by East-Asiatic waterfowl, of which we have had the Green-head Pochard (*Nyroca bæri*) in numbers, the Dwarf Goose (*Anser erythropus*), the Bronze-Cap (*Eunetta falcata*) as above noted, and now this species, one of our very rarest visitants in the ordinary way.

That these birds had been habitually visiting us and had been overlooked, I do not for a moment believe. It is far more reasonable to suppose that they come at long intervals only or in very fluctuating numbers. A proof of this was furnished to me by Mr. W. Rutledge, who, in dealing in animals in Calcutta for forty years, had never had this Teal or the Bronze-Cap offered for sale by the natives, though he had imported specimens from China as fancy birds.

The Clucking Teal's chief peculiarity appears to be that to which it owes its name, its harsh and frequently repeated clucking call ; this is constantly being uttered by the males, and will very likely prove to be confined to that sex.

The Andaman Teal.

Nettium albigulare, BLANFORD, Faun. Brit. Ind., Birds, Vol. IV, p. 444.

VERNACULAR NAMES :—None known.

This is the largest of the genus, but has proportionally the smallest wings ; its bill is also short, like that of the Clucking Teal. The sexes are alike. The colour is a mottled brown, very dark, almost chocolate in fact. The throat, fore-neck, and a ring round the eye are white, as is a patch in front of the wing-bar, which is velvet-black with a longitudinal bronze-green streak in the middle, and a narrow lower border of white formed by the white edging of the first secondary.

The white on the head shows a tendency to spread, and in one Indian Museum specimen, a fine male, extends all over the surface ; possibly this is a matter of age, as old birds get white at the root of the beak. At any rate this variation is now quite common, and nearly all the living specimens I have seen brought from the Andamans show it. Such specimens have bred in the London Zoological Gardens, but their young were as described below, with no white on the face.

Young birds have no white round the eye.

The bill and feet are blue-grey and the eyes reddish-brown or red.

The male is about seventeen inches long, with a wing rather over seven-and-half, bill about one-and-three-quarters, and shank under one-and-half ; females are smaller.

The Andaman Teal is resident in the Islands from which it takes its name, but is not confined to the South Andaman alone, as has been supposed, for Captain A. R. S. Anderson, I.M.S., late Surgeon-Naturalist to the *Investigator*, states in his Report for 1897-98, page 7, that he found a flock on East Island, the most north-easterly of the group. It may also straggle occasionally to the mainland, as one, the fragments of which were sent to the Indian Museum, was recorded some years ago in *The Asian* from Burma, where it had been shot from among a flock of Whistlers.

This Teal frequents, in pairs or flocks, both fresh and salt water, apparently preferring the former. Unlike most of the Ducks of this section, it perches freely, and it is active both on land and water. I have seen some of the specimens in the Calcutta Zoo dive for food like Pochards ; it is not very timid, and has a peculiarly soft noiseless flight as I have been able to observe in unpinioned specimens at large in the London Zoo. I noticed that the drakes were very pugnacious ; they also assisted in the care of the young, unlike most of the typical Ducks. The note is a low whistle in the male and a quack in the female. The nest has been found in August ; it was made of grass and placed on the ground ; the egg is cream-coloured and smooth.

The Oceanic Teal.

Nettium gibberifrons, SALVADORI, Brit. Mus. Cat., Birds, Vol. XXVII, p. 255.

This Teal with which the Andaman Teal was formerly confused, is a widely-ranging species, found through the islands from Java to Australia and New Zealand. It has a close general resemblance to the Andaman Teal, but has a more speckled head, no white eye-ring at any age, and no white border to the first secondary quill. It lays about a dozen creamy-white eggs in holes in trees. In Australia there is another race or species (*Nettium castaneum*) in which, while the female is like both sexes of the sombrely coloured Oceanic Teal, the male has a very distinct plumage, the head being dark glossy-green, and the breast and flanks bay with black spots. This form has been known to stray to Java, so deserves mention here.

APPENDIX I.

SYNOPTICAL TABLE OF THE INDIAN ANATIDÆ.

THE DIAGNOSTIC CHARACTERS given in this table apply to the species as a whole, irrespective of age, sex or season.

FAMILY CHARACTER.

Ducks in the wide sense are web-footed water-fowl with a straight beak armed with teeth or ridges along the edges of both chaps.

SUB-FAMILY I.—SWANS (p. 8).

Size larger than tame Goose, neck exceedingly long, face bare.

Bare face pale—
Whooper (p. 11).

Bare face dark—
Mute Swan (p. 9).

SUB-FAMILY II.—GEESE (p. 14).

Size smaller than tame Goose, usually bigger than tame Duck nostrils central; plumage grey or brown, pale-barred.

Bill well over two inches; feet flesh-colour—
Gray Goose (p. 17).

Bill under two inches, black at root—
Pink-footed Goose (p. 19).

Bill two inches, feet orange—
White-fronted Goose (p. 20).

Bill well under two inches, feet orange, size hardly bigger than tame Duck—
Dwarf Goose (p. 21).

Plumage pale clear grey, with orange black-tipped bill—
Bar-headed Goose (p. 23).

Plumage very dark with white markings and red or buff breast—
Red-breasted Goose (p. 24).

SUB-FAMILY III.—MERGANSERS (p. 29).

Size that of tame Duck or smaller, bill toothed, tapering more than twice as broad at root as at tip.

Beak lead-colour, under two inches—
Smew (p. 35).

Beak reddish, well over two inches, with about eighteen teeth between nail and nostril—
Red-breasted Merganser (p. 33).

Beak reddish, well over two inches, with about fifteen teeth between nail and nostril.—
Goosander (p. 31).

SUB-FAMILY IV.—TRUE DUCKS (p. 38).

Size between tame Goose and Duck, generally smaller than tame Duck ; bill with lower chap shutting into upper ; sides generally parallel or getting wider towards the end, and nostrils (with one exception) nearer root of bill than tip.

SECTION A.—*Diving Ducks, with outer toe as long as middle or longer, and hind toe with a deep lobe or flap giving it a leaf-like outline* (p. 38).

1. Bill with nostril nearer tip than root—
Golden-eye (p. 42).

2. Bill normal, wing only about six inches from knuckle to tip—
Stiff-tail (p. 43).

3. Bill normal, wings well over seven inches, usually with a white bar.

Bill and feet more or less red or orange—
Red-crested Pochard (p. 45).

Wing with no white bar—
Common or Red-headed Pochard (p. 48).

Bill broadened at tip, greatest breadth equal to distance between nail and nostril ; no crest—
Scaup (p. 50).

Bill shaped as above, but a crest present—
Tufted Pochard (p. 51).

Bill not much broadened, crown chestnut or brown—
White-eyed Pochard (p. 55).

Bill not much broadened, crown dark green or blackish—
Green-headed Pochard (p. 53).

SECTION B.—*Walking or Perching Ducks, with outer toe shorter than the middle, hind toe with narrow lobe or none and bill about as long as shank* (p. 63).

1. Size very small, less than Pigeon, bill an inch long—
Cotton Teal (p. 74).

2. Size larger, quills short and not showing in closed wing.
Plumage mostly chestnut, with cream bar above tail—
Large Whistler (p. 66).
Plumage mostly dun, with maroon bar above tail—
Small Whistler (p. 65).

3. Size large, wings long-quilled, tips of quills showing plainly inclosed wing.
Plumage chestnut, with black-and-white wings—
Brahminy (p. 69).
Plumage white and black, with red or fleshy bill and feet—
Sheldrake (p. 70).

4. Wings dark, body mostly white—
Comb Duck (p. 72).

5. Bill short, small and French-grey or blue—
Wigeon (p. 78).

6. Tips of quills showing plainly inclosed wing, silver-grey on outer web, steel-blue or inner—
Mandarin Duck (p. 76).

SECTION C.—*Ordinary surface-feeding Ducks, with outer toe shorter than middle, hind toe with narrow lobe, bill markedly longer than shank* (p. 81).

1. Bill very long, twice as broad at tip as root—
Shoveller (p. 88).

2. Bill ordinary, tail long and pointed—
Pintail (p. 90).

3. Bill and tail ordinary, wing nine inches or over.
Wing-bar French-grey—
Wood-duck (p. 83).
Wing-bar fawn—
Pink-head (p. 84).
Wing-bar metallic green, with a white border and long white splash above—
Spotted-bill (p. 94).
Wing-bar steel-blue, outside of inner quills of wing tipped white—
Yellow-nib (p. 96).
Wing-bar steel-blue, with white borders only—
Mallard (p. 92).
Wing-bar white—
Gadwall (p. 98).

Wing-bar black—

Bronze-cap (p. 99).

4. Bill and tail ordinary, wing 8½ inches or under.

Plumage grey-brown and whitish, no wing-bar, silver-grey edging to quills—

Marbled Teal (p. 86).

Bill with fringing showing below upper chap, wing-bar light dull green or none—

Blue-winged Teal (p. 101).

Wing-bar cinnamon, green, black and white in succession—

Clucking Teal (p. 106).

Wing-bar white or buff and white in front, then half black and half green—

Common Teal (p. 104).

Wing-bar velvet-black, with a longitudinal bronze streak and large white patch in front—

Andaman Teal (p. 108).